Ex Líbrís

THE PYRAMID
AND THE URN

William Lawrence, by Johann Kerseboom

THE PYRAMID AND THE URN

The Life in Letters of a Restoration Squire:
William Lawrence of Shurdington, 1636–1697

EDITED AND ILLUSTRATED BY
IONA SINCLAIR

ALAN SUTTON PUBLISHING LIMITED

First published in the United Kingdom in 1994 by
Alan Sutton Publishing Ltd
Phoenix Mill · Far Thrupp · Stroud · Gloucestershire

First published in the United States of America in 1994 by
Alan Sutton Publishing Inc · 83 Washington Street · Dover NH 03820

British Library Cataloguing in Publication Data

A catalogue record for this book is available from the British Library.

ISBN 0 –7509–0765–7

Library of Congress Cataloging in Publication Data
applied for

Jacket illustration: Johannes Kip's print of Shurdington (courtesy of Mr A.M.
Elliott, The Greenway Hotel, Shurdington).

Typeset in 10/12 Palatino
Typesetting and origination by
Alan Sutton Publishing Ltd
Printed in Great Britain by
The Bath Press, Avon.

Contents

Part II

Note
The New Year began on March 25th so letters dated between January 1st and March 25th have been given the year, according to modern dating, in square brackets. By the 1690s, William Lawrence himself often gave the second date – as, for instance, 1691/2.

Illustrations

Foreword

The text which I edited under the title *The Diary of William Lawrence*, published in 1961 by the antiquarian bookseller and collector, J. Stevens-Cox, has long been out of print. Moreover my friend Iona Sinclair has had access to numerous Lawrence items which were not in the Stevens-Cox manuscript volume. I am therefore delighted that she and her publisher, Alan Sutton Publishing, have now done fuller justice to William Lawrence. He deserves to be more widely known. Although hardly a great poet, the best of his prose rises to almost poetic heights, as we follow his tragic evolution from the young man castigating and satirising republicans and religious hypocrites to the dessicated old Whig saddened and embittered by bereavement.

This attractively-produced volume may be commended to all those who are interested in the seventeenth century, and indeed to anyone who wishes to get inside the mind of the past. For here we see the world through the eyes of someone living three hundred years ago, gifted yet desperately vulnerable. Whatever is sometimes meant by the phrase 'human interest', it is surely present here in ample measure.

Gerald Aylmer

Acknowledgements

The letters of William Lawrence in the custody of the Oriental and India Office Collections (MSS Eur E 387B) appear by courtesy of the Board of the British Library. The quotations from the *Diary* manuscript of William Lawrence's writings appear by kind permission of Mr Gregory Stevens-Cox of Guernsey. They were previously published as *The Diary of William Lawrence* by the Toucan Press, Beaminster, 1961, edited by Professor G.E. Aylmer who kindly agreed to the inclusion here of several passages and letters from the *Diary*.

I also gratefully acknowledge the help given by the staff of the Public Record Office, the House of Lords Record Office, the National Library of Wales, the Museum and Library Services of Gloucestershire, Hereford, Hampshire, Wiltshire and Oxfordshire County Councils, the Museum and Library of Maryland History and the Honourable Society of the Middle Temple.

I particularly thank Mr Anthony Elliott of the superb Greenway Hotel, Shurdington, for his interest and the loan of the Johannes Kip drawing and print for inclusion in the book and on the jacket cover. Among many individuals who helped establish parts of the 'jigsaw puzzle' of information, I would like especially to thank Mr Jamie Findlay for his help in researching Judge William Powlett, Major General Michael Hicks for his help in establishing the life of Sir Michael Hicks and Dr Christopher Thacker for his generous assessment of the special nature of William Lawrence's memorial garden. To several people are owed my unbounded thanks and sense of indebtedness: Professor Gerald Aylmer, formerly Master of St Peter's College, Oxford, who added to his other kindnesses by contibuting a foreword, the military historian, John Strawson and those members of my family whose encouragement alone led to the publication of William Lawrence's letters. The Senior Editor at Alan Sutton Publishing, Fiona Latham, was a delight to work with and I thank her for her care and diligence in helping to shape the final form of the book and for her enthusiasm for William Lawrence and his letters.

Most especially, I owe a tremendous debt of gratitude to Dr Neil O'Sullivan, formerly of St John's College, Cambridge and now of the Department of Classics and Ancient History of the University of Western Australia for undertaking the painstaking task of translating and attributing the classical quotations so willingly and skilfully.

I.S.

This book is dedicated to the memory of my father who loved Shurdington.

Introduction

These letters tell the story of one man, William Lawrence, and his world – the England of the second half of the seventeenth century.

William Lawrence was born on February 12th, 1636 or 7,[1] and grew up in Hackney, then a market-garden village outside London. His father, Anthony – an apparently unsuccessful merchant – was one of three sons of a landowner with an estate at Shurdington in Gloucestershire. William Lawrence was educated at the expense of his uncle, also William, and, although his name does not appear in the University records, he writes of going to 'college' during the Interregnum. There he would have read the classics, logic, rhetoric, history, theology and modern languages to equip him for the role of the current ideal of the 'gentleman scholar'. In 1654 he entered Gray's Inn to read Law, later transferring to the Middle Temple. He was called to the Bar in 1662.

It is as a young law-student in 1659 that we first meet William Lawrence – clever, somewhat precocious and touchy. The four letters of this date show an already developed irreverence for authority, whether as members of his own family or the public figures of the day. He had, at the same time, a gift for friendship and evoked a loyal and compassionate devotion from his friends. He reserved his deeply abiding love for three people – his younger brother, Isaac and, later, his wife, Anne, and only son, Willy. The relationship with all three seems to have been idyllic.

Lawrence's deepest problem stemmed from the fact that, while he was acutely short of money for most of his life, he was apparently spoilt by the prospect of affluence before him. His bachelor uncle, William (who had himself inherited the estate in Gloucestershire in 1638), made Lawrence his heir and the inheritance of Shurdington ('my little Canaan') became his main preoccupation. Years of frustration followed while his uncle refused to oblige him by dying.

The family were intensely proud of their lineage, tracing their descent from a twelfth-century Sir Robert Lawrence of Lancashire. The family's combined hope was that through William Lawrence and his son, Willy, the family would be restored to its 'ancient splendour'. These letters are a record of that endeavour. To this end, according to Lawrence, his uncle remained single and his brother, Isaac, who, as a younger son, had been 'bred a merchant', travelled to 'gaine wealth'. It was, perhaps, Lawrence's failing

---

1 Lawrence mentions his date of birth in one of the (unpublished) letters – the year is deduced from the text. No record of his birth or baptism has been found.

THE LAWRENCE FAMILY

Sir Robert Lawrence (knighted 1191)

Sir Robert L. m. a dau. of James Trafford — of Lancashire

James L. m. Mathilda, dau. of John Washington — " "

John L. m. Margaret, dau. of Walter Chessford — " "

John L. m. Elizabeth Holt — " "

Sir Robert L. m. Margaret Holden — " "

Sir Robert L. knighted 1454 m. Amphilis Longford — " "

Sir James L. m. Cecily Boteler

Sir Thomas L. m. Lady Eleanor Welles

Sir John L.

Sir John L. m. Lady Grizel Gibbon (of Iver, Bucks. & Chelsea)

Sir John L. Bt.

Sir Thomas L. Bt m. Anne Inglish
1645–1714

Thomas –1701 Harry

Robert Lawrence m. Margaret Lawrence of Lancs

Sir Robert L. m. dau. of Thos. Stanley   John L.

William L. –1588 m. 1. Isabel Molineux
                        2. Alice of Withington b. 1509

Robert L. 1513–82 m. Eleanor Stratford
(he bought the Manor of Shurdington)

William 1565–1638 m. Margaret Higford   Robert –1643   Anthony –1645
(of Shurdington who built the house)   (of Oldiswell)   (of Withington)

William   Anthony m. Barbara Taylor   Issac m. Grizel   Thomas –1691 William
1594–1682 1606–70   –1662   1614–84

James Martin

John Bigge m. Catherine Anne   William m. 2. Dulcibella   Issac   Jane m. 1. Henry Wood
            –1683   1650–91 1636/7–97 1658–1736   1639–79   2. Robert Hudson
                                                                                 3. John Wright

William

Compiled from: *The Diary of William Lawrence*, *Burke's Extinct and Dormant Baronetcies*, *Visitations to Gloucestershire 1682–3* (Exeter 1804 Fenwick & Metcalfe), Parish Registers and the Text.

PART I

'I should be proud and pleased to divert your perhaps tired thoughts; and if I can waste some of your solitary minutes, I shall think I both honour and improve my own.'

From William Lawrence's letter to Sir Richard Harrison.

LETTER 1

Lawrence opens his letter-book with four letters written as a young man, while he was a student at the Middle Temple. All are written in 1659, a year of turmoil following the death of Oliver Cromwell. One letter describes these events; the other three his own problems. The first of the latter shows Lawrence in a tetchy and not very attractive light. He is short of money and ready to blame his relations for his difficulties: the cousin to whom he is writing is censured for his neglect and his aunt for being too tight with her money. His dissatisfaction is only partially relieved by his luck at dice.

Since Lawrence cannot have been proud of this letter, it says much for his honesty – or perhaps for his amusement at its inconsequence – that he included it in the collection of his letters, made nearly forty years later.

The letter is dated January 1658. As the New Year began on March 25th, this would now read 1659.

LETTER 1

For Mr G.L.   January 4th 1658[9]

Cousin,

I should have been glad if either I had so much interest in you, or you so much freedom from your other affairs, as might have served for the production of a letter; for methinks neither your mistress nor your Maker, neither love nor religion, can so distract your memory as not to let one thought peep this way. . . .

My Aunt's table I confess is very free and open, but her money lies too close in the chest, she had rather see it all swallowed than any lent; she is ready to feed her friends when they don't want her, and starve them when they do.[1] 'Tis true my bond was of no force being yet under age, and perhaps she would not venture to oblige me, because I could not oblige myself. But yet methinks my relation might have answered that sorry doubt and have supplied the want of time.

But Cousin, what I missed from the living, I found from the dead; I was casually at an ordinary [eating-house] where I heard the bones of some old cinq-quater [gamester] rattle in the boxes; I changed two broad pieces and from a sudden thought of success, boldly set my self down to In and In.[2]

---

1 The word 'friend' was also used of a relation in the 17th century. The aunt may well have been Grizel, wife of his father's younger brother, Isaac.
2 A gambling game played with dice.

And then fortune either to debauch or oblige me, declared so effectually on my side that I never saw silver run so quick into one hand. Several battles were successfully fought and soon decided; so that I immediately raised a very good fund; and then, being not a little jealous of the jilt, I suddenly gave off, and resolved never to court or trust her more.

. . .

Your Servant

W.L.

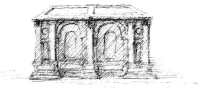

'her money lies too close in the chest'

LETTER 2

INTRODUCTION

The second letter, written four months later, is of a very different kind. William Lawrence is writing to his brother, Isaac, who has been travelling to Syria and Egypt and is, at present, in Greece. It is one of the few letters concerned almost entirely with historical events. It is also the longest and the most complex – for which reason it is abridged here and the full text given in Appendix B.

It is eight months since Cromwell's death and the country is in a state of anarchy. The letter, appropriate to the theme, is written in satirical vein and Lawrence, sensibly, refers his brother 'to the print for a more solid information'.

Briefly: a power struggle between Parliament and the Army had developed at the end of the Civil War. In 1648, the Army had purged Parliament of its more moderate (Presbyterian) members and the 50 radical (Independent) members who remained – known as the Rump Parliament – voted for the trial of Charles I, resulting in his execution. Four years later, Cromwell abolished the Rump at sword-point, telling them they had 'sat long enough' – ending a 4-year period of republicanism that was seen, in 1659, as the 'Good Old Cause'.

Cromwell subsequently assumed the title of 'Lord Protector' – King in all but name – and experimented with various forms of civil government (both elected and nominated) and by direct military rule.

Cromwell's death, in September 1658, was followed by a short calm, before the stormy events of 1659, the first three months of which this letter describes. Cromwell was succeeded as Lord Protector by his ineffectual son, Richard, (known to history as 'Tumbledown Dick'). He could not control, as his father had done, the many disparate elements that had made up the Parliamentary side in the Civil War, and who had been bound only by their political or religious grievances against Charles I.

Two months after Cromwell's death, Richard Cromwell called for elections in order to obtain money with which to pay the Army. The new Parliament first sat at the end of January but the three main differing power factions, of Protector, Army and Republicans, made peaceful government impossible. Parliament was dissolved in April when Generals Fleetwood and Desborough (Cromwell's son-in-law and brother-in-law respectively) staged a military coup. At the beginning of May, the month of this letter, Richard was forced to resign as Lord Protector – an office which he said had become a 'burden' to him. He was heavily in debt and later fled the Country.

A group of Army officers and Republicans insisted on the recall of the old Long Parliament (originated in Charles I's time) which first sat on 8th May. The Presbyterians were again refused admittance so that this Parliament became a second 'Rump', dedicated to the 'Good Old Cause' of republicanism which, 'divers Citizens of London' proclaimed, was 'the Lord's doing and was marvellous in their Eyes'.[3] It was not a view shared by William Lawrence.

---

3 *House of Commons Journals* VII, 9th May 1659.

William Lawrence is 22 or 23, his brother, Isaac, a merchant in the Mediterranean and Levant, is 19. Lawrence opens by apologizing for his dilatoriness in writing to his brother – which sounds as lame as such excuses usually do.

LETTER 2

To my Brother Isaac Lawrence, at Argive [Argos]   May 30th 1659

Dear Brother,

Had I closely pursued the respects due from nature and example I should have returned as many letters as I have received, but the distance is so great, and the conveyance so confused, that it is very hard to reach you.

Argive hath been an old enemy and almost always in arms against our trade and our religion; she hath been guilty of a long piracy, and her shores formerly polluted with the lamentable shipwreck of the Spanish Navy;[4] and to make the scale more heavy I may throw in my own wrongs: she now robs me of your society, and steals away that blessing to which I have a natural as well as a civil right.

By my last I sent you the news then in being, and that you may see how small a time may give birth to many great revolutions. I give you a satirical taste of what hath happened since, and refer you to the print for a more solid information.

The Army, that military hydra, have made a dreadful change, and cast the affairs of the Nation into a new mould; the face of Government is ruined, the Parliament dissolved, and our new Protector levelled again into his old private fortune. They stand up for the Good Old Cause [of republicanism], as good indeed as old, for 'tis an infant within age, receiving its birth but in '48, when their rage ran high, broke all the bonds of law and religion, and made Majesty shamefully bleed and expire. This spurious brat, this son of confusion, was nursed up for four years [1648–53], and then turned out for an impertinent useless thing: after this it wandered about the Nation like a vagabond meeting neither with pity nor relief; at last the poor fool being almost starved and under the lash of a severe Government, fled to the Army for protection; whose officers full of guilt and fears, receive this sorry brat, this Good Old Cause, fed and clothed him in many gay colours, gave him a house to live in and some careful tutors, whom they call by the name of the Long Parliament. They would persuade the world that he is very gentle and innocent, but to me he looks as fierce as a cannibal; for things seem to be in a very tragic

---

4 Greece was part of the Ottoman Empire. The reference is to Turkish attacks on the merchant shipping of the Western States and the taking of their sailors as Christian slaves. The English Navy had been weak under Charles I but the piracy was largely ended by the stronger Commonwealth Navy.

condition, tending to blows and blood, and hastily running into their first confusion.

The Nation is so trampled upon by Troopers, and so submissive to the force of powder, that every single nine-penny Redcoat[5] thinks he can discharge a parliament with as much ease as his musket. Faux's [Guy Fawkes'] treason seems to be now revived; what he designed, these execute; he prepared a blow, but these give it. In this they agree, they both put their powder in barrels; but then in this they differ, the Army acts with much greater impudence; for he hid his powder, but these shake their barrels and openly show it. 'Tis well they are shut up in an island for else they would shake the whole body of nature, and put the universal frame into disorder and confusion. The Praetorian bands, the Mamalukes, the Janissaries[6] were like to these soldiers in all things but their pride and insolence, in which they are not to be equalled, unless by their more natural protector the Governor of Hell, that strong garrison of Redcoats. There is not a face among 'um but abounds in brass; I believe they are out of God's protection, and that when he looks upon the Nation he holds his hand between his eye and the Army, else such successive sins could not lie so long unrevenged . . .

. . . There have been of late years so many changes and such antipodes in government, that I think no age or nation hath been so eminently wicked as to be able to produce a parallel; and yet there are still such abundance of ill-humours in the fanatic heads of our new masters, and the disease so very averse to a solid cure, that I fear a vein must be once more opened, and we must at last bleed into a better temper . . .

They have made the Protector [Richard Cromwell] less than a Roy d'Yvidot,[7] and stripped him of all his honours; his fortune halts as well as he. Usurped dominions must be kept by the same means they were acquired; his father left him his throne but not his courage; he was lost for want of resolution, and his loss is therefore the greater, because 'tis thought that, upon consideration of a legal right in a restless party and that no violent things are perpetual, he was inclined to satisfy the hopes of many by a fair resignation. Weeping Fleetwood was persuaded to head the revolution, he hath the greater power but Lambert the greater craft, who 'tis said, endeavours to possess all, by the more secret arts of divide and reign: which is a principle which may perhaps serve a present turn, but must at last undo the whole party . . . [8]

5 Cromwell's infantry had first appeared in red coats in 1645.
6 The bodyguards, respectively, of the rulers of Rome, Egypt and Turkey, all of whom came to exercise great political influence and all of whom deposed their lawful rulers.
7 Approximately 'King of the Castle'. From the 14th–16th centuries, all free-holders of the town of Yvetot (near Rouen) were, by custom, styled 'Kings'. (There was a later, 19th century, song: 'le Roi d'Yvetot'.)
8 Lieutenant General Charles Fleetwood, the overall commander of the Army, and Major General John Lambert, the commander of the Army in England who, it was thought, hoped to succeed Cromwell. (Fleetwood was known for his tendency to weep in public.)

It will be three years before I can reach the Bar, and therefore I don't much care though the pockets of the subject be poor and their tongues at peace: but when that time is expired, I shall begin to pray that God would send much money and many quarrels. My Uncle is not yet turned marble,[9] which makes me for the present ill at ease [financially]; but my physicians tell me I might certainly recover could I get into my possession a good dose of aurum potabile [drinkable gold],[10] or two or three bushels of the King's pictures.[11]

If your stay at Argive shall be continued, and shall give you a prospect of much profit and little danger, I hope all things will so succeed to your desires and mine, that your felicity and years may have an equal progress, and that the blessings of heaven upon you may be as thick and numerous as are the daily wishes of

Your most affectionate brother

W.L.

*'His father left him his throne
but not his courage.'*
Richard Cromwell by Robert
Walker.

---

9 William Lawrence, senior, who has made Lawrence his heir – a circumstance which makes this an outrageous remark.
10 Drinking powdered gold was thought to cure disease.
11 The Royal collection was largely sold to provide funds for the Commonwealth Government.

POST-SCRIPT TO LETTER 2

General Lambert later dissolved the Rump Parliament and marched north to confront General Monk, the commander of the Army in Scotland, who had declared his support for the Rump. Lawrence's suggestion that a 'vein must be once more opened' was nearly realized but a severe winter and lack of pay for Lambert's troops, resulted in wholesale desertions and renewed Civil War was averted.

In January, General Monk brought his army south and reinstated the Presbyterian (moderate and, by now, pro-royalist) members in the House of Commons. This Parliament voted for new elections to form a Parliament which, in turn, voted for the restoration of the Monarchy.

On 29th May 1660 – a year, less a day, after the writing of this letter – King Charles II was welcomed back by the vast majority of his subjects.

'Fleetwood . . . hath the greater power but Lambert the greater craft.'
Lieutenant General Charles Fleetwood and Major General John Lambert

LETTERS 3 & 4

INTRODUCTION

Lawrence is in explosive mood again. A friend has spread gossip about him and he dreads that it will come to the ears of his uncle. It becomes apparent that, although William Lawrence, senior, has made Lawrence his heir, there is no formal agreement. William, senior, is a bachelor but has more than one nephew, any one of whom could be made heir to his estate at Shurdington.

The *Diary* contains some love poems ('A Lament', 'Amyntas courts Amaryllis to a kiss' and 'Amyntas and Amaryllis mutually embrace') dating from 1658 or 9, which may be descriptive of the affair suggested in this letter – and the implied subject of the gossip.

Quoting briefly from all three poems it is possible to follow the course of the affair:

Describing himself, in the person of Amyntas, as a 'jolly swain, with mirth not meanly stored' . . . he writes of Amaryllis with distant admiration, yet:

> One victory contents her not
> She sets mankind on fire.

He approaches in the second poem:

> Come and be coy no more, my Fair,
> Let love not suffer this eclipse.

and succeeds in the third:

> Some fancies rove,
> Talking of chains and strange conceits in love
> But if these snowy arms love's fetters be,
> Heaven make me an eternal slave,
> And rather kill than set me free.

This remains an affair Lawrence does *not* wish to reach the ears of his uncle.

LETTER 3

For W.H.[12]   June 27th 1659

. . . When a man's reputation is spotted, it is a stain for ever and never recovers its complexion. . . . You had little reason, justice, friendship, or humanity, to rip up my supposed secrets and lay open the courser parts of my life; especially in matters wherein no witnesses are admitted, and have

---

12 Possibly a cousin, William Higson, whose home, at Badgeworth, in Gloucestershire was 2 miles from that of Lawrence's uncle, William Lawrence, at Shurdington.

usually more of conjecture than truth. It makes me almost think that there is no society in nature beyond that of acquaintance and that the appellation of friend is but an idle title, a thing that hath a name but no being, and (as if it shared nature's with the hyena's voice) allures only to betray.

Perhaps (and I believe it) the late affront given you by Mrs R. first moved your gall and raised up that bitter discourse; but you may know that women are wasps and will sting; their tongues are their ablest, if not their only weapons, and always whetted and fit for service; it is not our province to brawl, nor theirs to fight; and therefore when they take the liberty to expose us, I think a patient slight is much better than a railing revenge. But, admit your passion to be just against her, must it therefore follow that my forehead must be branded with infamy for another's wrongs, and because she offends, must I suffer? . . .

I have some relations whose interest makes them as watchful as Argus, their heads are full of eyes, and those eyes always open:[13] every little slip is magnified, and every step I make is observed and censured. My fortunes (you know) are not upon force but liking; I may as well be styled haeres factus as haeres natus ['made heir as born heir'] owing as much to adoption as nature; insomuch that there lies no certainty in my hopes, and my arbitrary title is to be secured as well by my merit as my blood. So that he who wounds my reputation, makes a dangerous thrust at my fortune, and may perhaps shake that steady and liberal hand which supports it. And this (for ought you know) may be the event of your weak and wild reflections.

But of this enough. I have delivered my sentiments, and now wait for yours.

W.L.

LETTER 4

[To the same] July 9th 1659

Though I had entertained a very hard opinion of your casual discourse being too openly delivered, yet I was not so settled as to be beyond the command of reason. I could not upon second and more serious thoughts imagine it a designed injury, nor did I so much resent the thing as fear the consequences. For the erratas of life grow by relation, and it is not everyman's discretion to make examination the preface to their belief.

Besides you know that although I have a natural, yet I have not an absolute right; my fortunes are precarious and hang upon the pleasure of another. And though the slips of youth and the errors of complexion may

---

13 Argus was the mythical son of Arestor. He was all-seeing, having 100 eyes, of which only two slept at a time.

(one would think) be easily over-looked or forgiven, yet youth and age see with different eyes, and that which is here a jest, is there a crime: their years being governed by such a severe folly that they expect discretion in cradles, and that wisdom should enter with our being; as if it owed more to generation than experience; and were rather the gift of nature than of time. They think, that, when they have added to their decayed lights another pair of eyes, they can see much farther than younger men: and then (which hath been your case and may be mine) their great gravity like those half glasses, swells the print, and makes every little letter, every small error in youth, to be no less than capital. They have the purse and the power to back their opinion, and therefore claim it as their right to judge and decree as they please. . . .

And now that this tide of words may shrink into its proper banks, and no longer swell beyond the just limits of amity, I give an eternal farewell to this theme, and hope you will kindly echo back those syllables wherein I again own and subscribe myself

your real friend

W.L.

'when they have added to their
decayed lights another pair
of eyes'

LETTER 5

Two years after the Restoration, Charles II is at the height of his popularity. 'Were you here,' Lawrence wrote, for instance, to his brother 'you might now see learning gather life again and flourish under the guard of Majesty' – a reference to the King's patronage of the Royal Society.

Isaac had returned from Greece but, in 1662, had set out again for Italy and Algiers. Lawrence writes what he calls a 'jocular' letter to his brother, when parsons are the chief victims of his irreverent pen.

Before the Restoration, Charles II had issued the Declaration of Breda, promising toleration in religious worship – to the Roman Catholics as well as the many puritan sects. To further this aim, there had been an attempt to find 'accommodation' between the Church of England and the Presbyterian Church. (The idea failed when the Presbyterians claimed they were given too little and the Church of England claimed it was asked to concede too much.) The Royalist, and predominantly Church of England, Restoration parliament had reversed the Declaration of Breda, passed the Act of Uniformity – requiring all parsons to have episcopal ordination – and the 1662 prayer book was commissioned to define the established church's forms of worship. Lawrence refers to the plight of the Presbyterian ministers, over a thousand of whom had, that week, been deprived of their livings.

'You might now see learning . . . flourish
under the guard of Majesty'
by W. Hollar from the frontispiece of the
History of the Royal Society

LETTER 5

For Isaac Lawrence   August 29th 1662

My dear Brother,

. . . The habit of a Levite [parson] is a cassock and a girdle, upon his head he wears a hat at large, the crown of it being bigger than a church bucket[14] and the brims spreading as wide as an umbrella. If my business calls me out when it rains, I usually take a parson with me to save the expense of a coach; for I can walk very dry under the eaves of his hat, and still find it as secure as a penthouse.[15] I was t'other day with one Parson Bruton, whose hat was so unreasonably large, that I could not be satisfied till I had handled it; for I was verily persuaded that the crown, like a steeple, was hung with bells; and that, as a hen doth her chickens, when he had a mind to warm his parishioners with the zeal of his doctrine, he used to shake his head a little and so chime his congregation under the brims.

I will now tell you a pleasant and true story of Parson White, his girdle, as is usual, hath two great tassels, and passing drunk through the Strand in the open day, he went to piss against the wall of Exeter House; but instead of his member he holds forth one of his tassels: the stream ran plentifully down his breeches, and when he had discharged his bladder of the burden, he very decently shook his tassle, and put it up instead of his bauble.

But while the fat of the land hangs very thick about the bellies of the orthodox clergy, the lamentable Presbyter looks very lean, and is indeed turned Independent, having nothing to trust to: the Quaker and all the petty prophets begin to foresee their fall, and the whole crew of new lights which have thus long rambled about the lower region and misled many, are themselves lost: their opinions, like thin exhalations, being too slight and empty to burn long.

St Bartholomew is now struck out of their calendar;[16] for very sad was the business of Sunday last, when the mournful Presbyter took leave of his Brethren: many gales of sighs issued from their religious lungs and the churches were so wet with the tears of the Saints, that one might have stood up to the ankles in holy brine. Much weeping and howling there was, had there been but gnashing of teeth too (but their tears they might show, their

---

14 In which water was stored, for public use, before the invention of fire-engines.
15 A lean-to shelter.
16 St Bartholomew's day (Sunday, 24th August) was the last day on which the Presbyterian ministers were permitted to preach.

Like many merchants' and lawyers' families, the Lawrences may well have been, at least, sympathetic to the Presbyterians. In letter 2b he calls Presbyterianism the 'older and better Cause'.

teeth they durst not) one of the wicked might have supposed a Hell in their divinity. I verily believe there was more salt dropped that day from their pious eyes, than would have pickled up all the herrings in the Nation. Mr Lye with his almighty lungs took a long farewell: in the morning he caused many a joint to be over-roasted; and in the afternoon it was six o'clock before he could part with his Dearly Beloved; at which time, bathed in sweat and tears, he bid adieu to his sacred function.

*'I can walk very dry under the eaves of
his hat'*

LETTERS 6 & 7

INTRODUCTION

The following year Lawrence writes to an un-named married woman, whose hand he had himself first sought ('I first began to spin the thread, though another had the felicity to tie the knot'). That their 'obedience was rather an act of fortune than inclination' suggests that Lawrence's prospects were not considered certain enough to satisfy a potential father-in-law.

The letters are dated 1663 – the year after Lawrence had been called to the Bar from the Middle Temple.

LETTER 6

For —   July 10th 1663

Believe me, Madam, those happy lines you sent me, being dictated by so bright a soul and drawn by so fair a hand, did so surprise and charm my senses, that I was a while fixed in the admiration of your generous temper and how absolutely unfit I was to be the subject of so many obliging characters. . . . I say, Madam, while I thus contemplate your great goodness and my own happy condition, I spread a net upon my soul and my thoughts which way soever they turn are entangled; for the one is too infinite to be discovered, and the other too large to be described, so that in the former I am like to lose my reason, and in the latter my rhetoric.

Though I have presumed to give fresh motion to that affection which time has put to a stand, and to revive a flame which not only absence but other more melancholy reasons seemed to have raked up in ashes, yet you have justly thought it worthy of success, and have freely given it both your pardon and protection. You considered that our affection was at first rather violently torn insunder, then parted, and that our obedience was rather an act of fortune than inclination. So it was; and since it was so, surely that which had a lawful beginning may have a lawful progress, and ought to lose nothing of its existence, whatever it doth of its latitude. I resolutely kept one point, though I lost eleven; I was still ready to claim my right was good. Though I missed the possession; for I set out first, though another ran fastest; I first began to spin the thread, though another had the felicity to tie the knot.

But it is vain to use arguments to confirm that, which from the abundance of your excellent inclinations, you have so long preferred and now so justly allowed. And therefore I need only assure you, that I meet your affection with a heart full of fire and gratitude, and I will as soon quit my life as either wrong your love or resign my own . . .

Madam,

Your entirely affectionate and faithful Servant

W.L.

LETTER 7

To the same   August 17th 1663

. . . Madam, I could very readily comply with your invitation, but as yet I think it may be a little too early; for the vapours in his head being not fully settled, a sudden appearance may perhaps lead him into wild fancies. And though your affection may make you resolute, and prove a suffecent bulwark against that yellow rage, yet rather than you should do any thing for my sake which may either blemish your person or break your peace, I could be patiently divided from all the happiness of life, and be as miserable as your frown or the decrees of Heaven can make me.

I see small matters will easily blow up his jealousy, make him judge my civility my crime, and that I come not so much to visit your person, as to invade his right. But were he well read in our mutual innocence, his suspicion need oblige him no longer to double the guards: your clear thoughts being averse to anything that may stain their innocent freedom; and mine moving with such a just sense of your honour, that it is not possible they should commit treason against so clear a virtue. This evil spirit of jealousy is easily raised, but not so easily lost; like the lion, it sleeps with its eyes open; its slumbers are but a counterfeit rest; it is most watchful when we think it most secure.

And therefore, Madam, you may pass the same sentence upon my letters which you made me unwillingly execute upon your own; for fire, though it consume the paper, will be sure to preserve the secret . . .

W.L.

LETTER 8

INTRODUCTION

Lawrence's heart may have been full of 'fire and gratitude' but caution seems to have won the day. We hear no more of Madam —. Soon, however, more serious concerns were to overtake Lawrence – and the country.

The Bubonic Plague broke out in London in the Spring of 1665. All those who could, including the Court, left London that Summer – spreading the disease to the countryside. The Plague lasted until the following year and 100,000 people died in London alone – the numbers being published each week in Bills of Mortality. On 16th October 1665 Pepys writes: '. . . they tell me that in Westminster there is never a physician and but one apothecary left, all being dead . . . '. Many, in fact, had fled along with their patients but, despite losses in his own family not, it seems, Lawrence's friend, Dr N.B., from the City.

Lawrence writes of a 'private jurisdiction' which has left him short of money but we are not told what this is.

LETTER 8

For Dr N.B.   November 2nd 1665

Sir,

All the parts of your letter, except where they pointed at tragical relations, were truly welcome; for they infused spirit into those thoughts which began to faint and languish under a long exile: this tedious separation having put a damp upon all my pleasures, and made me at least solitary, if not sad. For I have summed up all the content I enjoy here, when I tell you, that though the public calamity and a private jurisdiction circumscribe my earthly part, yet my soul which is always active and unconfined, makes daily sallies to the divided friends, and either by fancy fetcheth intelligence, or by paper invites it. . . .

When I avoided the enemy by flight I little thought of your being left upon the forlorn; for my part I retreated when I saw such disorderly dying; when I saw people crowd into another world, striving, like the gentry at a new play, who should get into the pit first, as if they either aimed at the best place or feared want of room. When I saw such a general lop of mankind, when I saw Death run madly up and down threatening to fell the whole forest, and not only the shrubs [saplings] but the taller trees, as well the rich as the poor, bow to that fatal axe. When I saw death and the grave drive such a destructive bargain, and the citizens go off not singly and by retail, but by heaps and in gross. When I saw those very carts, which used to bring home their wares, now carry off their carcases; as if Oliver's punishment were revived, and men were hurried to execution after death.[17] When I saw great

---

17 Cromwell's body had been exhumed after the restoration, together with those of other regicides, and hung at Tyburn.

pits digged instead of graves, and those too lying open, as if death had two stings, and were not contented with bare killing, but must have the living also look upon the slaughter, and behold him not only as a destroyer, but as one who insulted and took a pride in his victory. I saw Dr Page wait upon his triumph, I saw his apothecary make one in the common sacrifice, and thought it very hard, that he who had long kept the officinam salutis [workshop of health] and made up so many compounds could not now be admitted to a composition.

'great pits digged'
From a Plague broadsheet

When I thus saw the leaders quit the field, I thought it high time to retire; and yet I seemed rather to avoid the place than the peril; for the sickness, sequebatur a tergo [following behind], trod on my heels, and was here almost as soon as I. Many in this and the neighbouring parishes died of that pagan disease, and well may I so call it, for none of those unhappy bodies were permitted to lie in consecrated earth, or to have any thing that might resemble a Christian funeral. That which gave them a livelihood while living, gave them a lodging when dead; for they were buried in their own grounds; which, had a stranger seen, he could have thought no less, than that they were so much in love with their own turf, that they had a mind to prevent the right of the next heir and keep the possession after death.

But the grave at last seems glutted with this intemperate diet, the Country is now free, and the City Bills [of mortality] decrease apace; which makes me hope that I shall speedily see the scattered limbs of society reunite themselves, and the wandering lines of friendship meet again in their usual centre, the City. And since you have observed the blood of the surviving ladies to be heated with a strong appetite of union; and that you are both desirous to take the opportunity and active to seek it, I may also hope to find you, at my return, grafted upon some fair and flourishing stock, which by the production of a numerous issue, may in some small measure repair the public loss, or at least fill up those breaches which have been made in your own family.

While these hopes, that is, to see you and to see you double, are working in my head, methinks my soul grows more clear and fine; the grosser parts seem to separate and subside, drawing off much of those heavy lees which have been long floating among the uneasy thoughts of

Your faithful friend and servant

W.L.

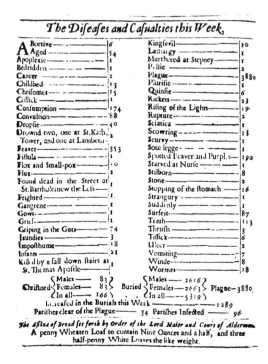

Bill of Mortality

LETTER 9

INTRODUCTION

Lawrence is now 29 or 30 and his uncle deems it time to be thinking of matrimony. William Lawrence, senior, has arranged a marriage for his nephew with the daughter of the Dean of Gloucester, making this possible by the promise of a generous marriage settlement. The Dean, however, has been dilatory in granting an interview with his daughter and Lawrence seems to be trying to enlist support from Saint Valentine – the letter is written on February 14th.

LETTER 9

To Dr Brough, Dean of Gloucester[18]   February 14th 1667[8]

Sir,

My fortune, as yet doubtful and suspected, doth shake my mind with such a confusion of thoughts, that I hope you will pardon me if I wait not for your voluntary summons but thus solicit for further information. To have writ sooner might perhaps have been not only a just act, but an expected civility, yet not knowing whether such hasty addresses might meet with your allowance, I thought it better thus long to spin out my expectations, and rather waive a duty than create a trouble.

But, Sir, my uncle now writes to me to know what progress I have made in my suit; to which I answered, that I was often desirous to give the lady a visit, but that you had as often told me that she was as yet neither well nor willing to marry; and that you still pressed me to forbear my address till her health and her humour were both settled. The former may be a good reason of delay; the latter none; for I am almost confident that if my access may be free and her thoughts be not already fettered, this common aversion will soon wear away and expire. For since the lady hath never yet seen me, I can think it no other than the effect of her modesty, and not any personal dislike. For I assure you, if this should be the cause, I should neither want the justice to acknowledge my defects, nor the generosity to drop my petition; my design being only to persuade, not to persecute her virtue; and only to make her my mistress, not my martyr.

Believe me, Sir, I am so well pleased with the report of her great endowments both from nature and education, and (if she be to be

---

18 Dean Brough (–1671) was appointed Dean of Gloucester by Charles I, while the Court was at Oxford during the Civil War (although he could not take up his appointment until the Restoration). He was Chaplain-in-Ordinary to Charles I, accompanied Queen Henrietta Maria into exile during the Civil War and is buried at St George's Chapel, Windsor (of which he was a Canon).

(*DNB* and Thos. Dudley Fosbrooke: *An Original History of the City of Gloucester*)

conquered) should judge myself to be so rich in blessings and so happy above the common fate of men, that methinks an age of expectation were but a weak merit and a slender piece of service.

But it is a higher power must be satisfied, and he is earnest to know, whether on your part there be any further progress designed, or whether on hers there may be an affection admitted. For since my uncle and you without my preceding knowledge have long ago adjusted the whole matter, it is not only fit, but high time that I should receive from you, and you from her, a full resolution; that so my uneasy thoughts may be not only more quiet by being less divided, but that the perhaps better fortune of your daughter may not be too long suspended by a successless treaty.

Sir, if my wishes may have a happy event, and a strict obedience can put on the face of merit, that which is now desired may hereafter be deserved, for you shall always find me as well in practice as expression

Entirely at your Service,

W.L.

LETTER 10

Sir,

I thought my suit in love would have been like a suit in Chancery, upon which I must have spent much money and time, and have been always perplexed and pestered with new orders without any signs of a final decree. My desired visits were still put off to another day, so that I could never come to a full hearing, nor meet with any accident that might either promise success or presage a dismission.

But chance hath at last outdone my curiosity, and I have now accidentally found out the true cause of these long delays. Her father would often tell me that he was very cordial in the matter, but that the indisposition of his daughter was so great, that it was no proper time for my address; yet at last he said she was pretty well, and thereupon admitted me to two short visits; and then again desired me to forbear till he should give me further notice, for she was fallen into a relapse.

But in the mean time and for the convenience of her recovery he takes lodgings for her at a scriveners in the Strand, who coming to ask my advice in a matter of law, casually (among other discourse) pitied a fine young lady who was kept at his house in a dark room and under a course of physic; and at my request he named the person. Upon which I told him the whole affair, and desired he would give me leave to see her; to which he consented. I was admitted into her chamber, and there she at last told me all that I desired to know; which was, that Sir J.C. had privately made his court to her; that among other things he gave her a pair of bracelets, which she found to be a violent charm; for when she put 'um on she had a great esteem for him, but when she put 'um off her thoughts were very indifferent. That her father looked upon his estate and his humour to be too light, and was therefore so very averse, that he banished him and confined her. That this severity had discomposed her to such a degree, that she was thought fit for the care of physicians, and was lodged there for that purpose. That she had submitted to the loss of her hair, and the unkindness of a dark room. That she always showed herself willing to take their physic, and took some, that she might with less suspicion throw the rest away. That her father had taken away her bracelets, whereby the charm was at an end, and that she had now no further regard for the person who gave 'um.

Why then, Madam, said I, you may take me into your heart, for 'tis pity such fair lodgings should lie empty. She then said, if I grant you this request, will you grant me another. I asked her what it was. She told me she had a great desire to see foreign Countries, and I must not refuse to travel with her. I told her, I liked the motion, and when we had seen this world, I would, like another Alexander, weep that there were no more worlds to be surveyed.

23

But, Sir, having from these and many other fancies, found what I sought, I pressed the main no further, but gave her a short compliment, and retired.

Upon a narrower search, I find that the mother was mad and died so;[19] that her sister is mad, and that though she may be worth a great many thousands, yet her distemper being a lunacy by descent, I think her to be a match only fit for a madman. I need not tell you my opinion of her, for you had the first sight. Had her head been sound, her heart had been worth seeking.

But, Sir, it is now time to leave this for a nobler theme, and to go from that which is expired, to that which hath no end; I may forget my love but not my gratitude, for this is always waking and now doing what the eye of heaven hath already done, that is, distinctly surveying, and passing through the several signs of your great bounty and affection; which bright constellations I have found to be ever shining upon me with a full and open light; and then most clearly when the nights were darkest and when the great light of fortune did threaten to forsake me. You would have lessened your own light that I might shine the brighter; you would have taken the glory from your own head to have circled mine; you freely and without any invitation offered to settle upon me a great part of your estate; and secure a greater; and gave me a power to treat for a wife.

But since the lady's fever hath cooled mine, and I dare venture no further, I now break my staff and return my commission: having nothing to add, but that I truly describe my thoughts while I subscribe myself

Your most obedient, and grateful nephew,

W.L.

'she had submitted to the
loss of her hair'

---

19 At the beginning of the Civil War, Dean Brough was removed from his Living at Windsor by the Parliamentary Commission. He was 'also plundered and his wife and children turned out of doors'. His wife was said to have died of grief afterwards. (*DNB*)

LETTER 11

March 20th 1667[8]

Sir,

When you told me that your daughter was pretty well inclined to receive my address, and thereupon gave me the liberty of two short visits, I concluded the way to be so thoroughly cleared of thorns and briars, that my future addresses would have been all smooth and successful. But you now desire me not to renew my visits till she were a little better disposed, and that you would in the mean time solicit my uncle for a larger settlement. But your use of these windings and turnings would only continue the labyrinth and rather involve than decide this tedious suit.

But, Sir, that I may no longer haerere in cortice, that I may no longer stick in the bark and never reach the body, I must acquaint you, that to perfect her recovery you have lodged her at London with a client of mine, and that by that means what I could not discover at your house I have casually found out at his. You only showed me the jewel; I saw it was very bright and fitter for the Court than the cabinet, and was therefore resolved to know why it had been so long sullied and so carefully concealed. I boldly entered into her chamber, in which there was no light but her own; she pardoned my intrusion with much civility, and at last opened to me the whole history of her lunacy and restraint. Her delicate features, her pleasing air, and her soft and obliging temper, first laid upon me the charm of love, and now of compassion. But it is too sad a subject for my pen either to describe her condition or deplore my own: for I met with two sorrowful objects, a heart prepossessed and a head disturbed. I have acquainted my uncle with the whole matter, and his opinion is, that though she seemed to me to be pretty well recovered, yet I might either at that time meet with a lucid interval, or perhaps her distemper may have run in a blood, and then it may taint the whole channel, and posterity may long feel the unhappy effects.

The affections of young ladies if crossed are many times fatal, and it may be much better for you to indulge than ruin so fine a creature. The fortune you give is great and may be much greater. Let her enjoy the man (which with submission I think to be the best remedy) his love and title may perhaps settle her disturbed thoughts, and secure her from a future relapse.

Thus, Sir, I conclude my amour, being very sorry to see my hopes overthrown, and never likely to rise beyond the title of Sir,

Your faithful Servant.

W.L.

POST-SCRIPT TO LETTER 11

There is no record of Miss Brough's marrying Sir J.C. (or anyone else) in either Gloucester Cathedral or Beverstone Church, of which Dean Brough also held the living.

(*Gloucestershire Marriage Allegation 1637–1680*, ed. Brian Frith, Bristol and Gloucester Archaeological Society)

LETTER 12

King Charles II had been on the throne for eight years, but the honeymoon period with both Parliament and the electorate was over. The Court was criticized for its immorality – of which a particularly notorious example is given here – and, the previous year, the King had concluded an unsatisfactory two-year war with the United Netherlands, England's chief trading rival. (This was the second Dutch War – the first had been fought in Cromwell's time.) On 12th July 1667, Pepys had written in his diary: ' . . . here a prince come in with all the love and prayers and good liking of his people . . . hath lost all so soon.'

Lawrence criticizes the King for his reluctance to engage in war and certainly he had been against declaring war in 1664, preferring to settle the differences by negotiation and because to do so would involve the then Dutch allies, France and Denmark. In theory, the King and his ministers (nominees of the Crown) were responsible for defence and foreign policy. In practice he frequently had to bow to pressure from Parliament who held the purse-strings.

Lawrence's fear of Louis XIV, the absolute monarch of Europe's strongest land power, is typical of that felt generally in the Country. Throughout his reign, Louis negotiated and fought to extend his frontiers, particularly into the Spanish Netherlands (present-day Belgium).

There is no dedication, but the tone of the letter suggests that Lawrence may be writing for his uncle's censorious eyes.

LETTER 12

[To an un-named friend or relation]   [Undated. 1668]

Sir,

I hope my last came to your hand, and the sudden approach of this will confirm my reformation: there is now nothing wanting but your pardon and then I am cured beyond the danger of a relapse. But yet I doubt I am running from one extreme into another, and while I fly the Scylla I may split upon the Charybdis.[20] I fear my former offence will seem to be rather translated than reformed: there may be as much guilt from too many letters as from none; and whereas before I was too remiss, I may now be too troublesome.

I would many times give you an account of the intrigues of the Court, wherein to comment as well as relate, to lash as well as inform is the leachery of intelligence, and here is room enough for all the whips of a satirist; but it is neither decent nor safe to peep into the cabinets or pry too nicely into the amours of princes. Those who wear upon their heads the

---

20 The equal dangers, in Greek mythology, between the rock and the whirlpool off the coast of Sicily.

weight and cares of a crown, may be, if not allowed yet at least forgiven the faults of nature, and such as equally arise from power and complexion. But yet the royal example spreads too fast, and now the only stratagem of a great man is how to betray a beauty and undermine the chaste and the modest. These are the victories, these are the triumphs of the Court; they will boast more openly of a wife corrupted or a beauty subdued than their ancestors ever did to win a battle, storm a city, or force a camp.

The Countess of Sh[rewsbury] had a son lately born, it blushed at the light and died; it was interred with great solemnity in the Abbey and among the ancestors of the Duke of Bu[ckingham] vice now throws off the mask, and looks as bold as innocence: the wife first lost her honour, and then the husband his life, the Duke first stained his blood, and then spilt it.[21]

The French King's designs are yet a riddle, his councils, (as a flint doth fire) keep all in darkness, and are not to be discovered 'til the steel be drawn and he comes to blows. Quo cadat in dubio est omnique a parte timetur. [How it will turn out is doubtful and there is apprehension on all sides.][22]

George Villiers, 2nd Duke of
Buckingham, afterVerelst

21 On 17th January 1662, Pepys writes of the duel between the Duke of Buckingham and the Earl of Shrewsbury ' . . . and all about my Lady Shrewsbury, who . . . hath for a great while been a whore to the Duke of Buckingham and so her husband challenged him . . . '. Lord Shrewsbury was 'run through the body' and died later of his wound. George Villiers, 2nd Duke of Buckingham, was a childhood friend of Charles II and one of the ablest, but most unscrupulous, of men about the King. He was finally banished and Lady Shrewsbury retired to a convent in France.
22 Ovid, *Metamorphoses* 10, 374.

But our Senate will continue sitting 'til they see where the busy ambition of that monarch will fasten; while our own, too much softened by his long converse with the softer sex, seems so little inclined to the rough salutes of war, that like a kind neighbour, he will be apt to meet 'um with the wrong arms, not those that repulse an enemy, but those with which he embraces a mistress and a friend.

Were the hearts of princes free from the vices of lust and ambition, their lives would not be shortened by luxury, nor their subjects wasted by war, the world would lie in a calm and we might finish our days in peace; but this is not only the virtuous but the vain wish of

Sir

your faithful servant

W.L.

LETTER 13

On 24th September 1667, Lawrence married Anne, daughter of James Martin, a London apothecary. Lawrence was 31 or 32; Anne was 18. It was, or became, a love match and, in a later letter, Lawrence describes Anne as having 'Virtue, Beauty, great Wit, and Fidelity'. On 19th June the following year, Willy, their only child was born. Anne and Willy became, with Isaac, the three people in his life whom Lawrence loved with uncritical devotion. We do not know if the marriage was arranged by William Lawrence, senior. Certainly, it had his approval, since he made over the majority of his Gloucestershire estate at Shurdington and Badgeworth to Lawrence, on the marriage – although himself retaining a life interest.

As a countryman at heart, Lawrence writes to a friend of his dislike of London (a view shared by his monarch) where the four elements offend the five senses.

The second Dutch War, which had been fought against the background of the Plague year of 1665–6 and the great Fire of London of 1666, had ended after a humiliating defeat (although England retained New York, captured during the early stages of the War). For the first two years, the victories and defeats had been evenly balanced, but the initial generous grant of money for the Navy, voted by Parliament, had been exhausted and lack of funds had forced the King to lay up the larger ships of the Fleet, at Chatham, in 1667. Sheerness had been fortified and a chain laid across the river, at Chatham, in March. Despite these precautions, a Dutch Fleet, under de Ruyter, had sailed up the Medway in June, breaking through the chain, and capturing or burning many of the ships of the Navy – including its pride, the *Royal Charles*.

Again the letter may well be written to Lawrence's uncle. The 'family' referred to would be a usual way in which to describe the household.

LETTER 13

[To an un-named friend]   [Undated. 1668]

Sir,

I am grown quite weary of the City, where all the elements are vitiated, where there is neither good air, nor good fire, nor good water, nor good earth. The air is tainted by the fires of coal, the water polluted with dogs and vermin, and all the earth you see, is either hardened into pebbles, or baked into brick. If you light upon a tree, you shall find the bark sullied with smoke, and the leaves crisped and withered, dying with heat and buried in dust. In that place no sense is rightly gratified; the smell is offended, the ear disturbed, the eye confined, and the air so very gross that you may even taste and feel it. In a word, the City is a large smoky prison and all the senses wear fetters.

But to refresh those wearied organs, and give my strained lungs some liberty to breathe, I retired into the country and spent one month at Hurst.[23]

---

23 Near Reading, the home of Anne's sister and her husband.

It was there that I received your letter: my thoughts were damped at the first lines when you tell me that sickness had laid a long siege to almost your whole family; but they were soon revived when I understood that every fortress was so well defended by Nature and the careful skill of the Governor, that the battery was vain, a retreat sounded, and all the breaches repaired. And now I hope, that having received such a general repulse, she will judge the forts impregnable, and vex 'um with no future attacks.

'Tis said that we shall have no Fleet out this year, but shall quietly permit the sails of our neighbour Nations to be so puffed up and swell not more with air than pride to see the old moderators of marine affairs, the old proprietors and possessors of the dominion of the narrow seas, now grow faint and lie asleep in their docks. But there is a chain designed to be laid over Chatham River in that place where the Dutch formerly broke another with ease; which makes me think that perhaps the humour of Xerxes may be revived, and it is a chain intended not so much to bar an enemy as to fetter a river, and chastise it for the damage it permitted when it bore the Dutch to a triumph.[24]

But that chain of amity which you have fastened by so many strong links of obligation, will bear up against all opposers and even against the strength of time; no power can force or break the resolution I have taken to be without end or intermission,

Sir,

your faithful servant

W.L.

The *Royal Charles*

24 When the Persian King, Xerxes, invaded Greece, he constructed a bridge across the Dardanelles, which was washed away by the sea. In Greek legend, he inflicted three hundred lashes on the rebellious sea and cast chains of iron across it.

LETTER 14

INTRODUCTION

Lawrence did not practise as a barrister for long. We know from the *Diary* that he wrote to his uncle in 1672 that the Law was a profession in which ' . . . none can be eminent without great Labour, strong Abilities, and (which was yet worse) a long Expectation . . . '. Instead, he pursued 'some more exciting Hopes but these, being thwarted by unexpected Accidents, though they promised much, performed little . . . '. His childless uncle and benefactor, William, was then 78 and Lawrence seems to have been content to await (with impatience) his uncle's death – when he would inherit the estate at Shurdington.

The Lawrences left London for Hurst, in Berkshire, around 1670 and went to live with the Bigge family (Anne Lawrence's sister and her husband, John Bigge). The Bigges had been Parliamentarians in the Civil War and had, at this time, acquired Haines Hill (the estate of the former Secretary of State, Sir Francis Windebank) which they were able to keep at the Restoration.

The following letter is written to Dr Robert Fielding, a doctor and magistrate, who lives at Gloucester.

LETTER 14

To Dr Robert Fielding   [Undated. *c.* 1670]

As it is with all natural bodies, they unquietly submit to a forced motion, and are never at rest till they have attained their centre. So 'tis with me and my domestics, every year hath driven us under a new roof. I have gone from house to house, from the country to the City, and now at last from London to Hurst: from whence I shall wander no more, 'til the aged reversion drops and I shall come to possess the long-expected remains: for Sherington [Shurdington] is the end of my journey, and those but the several stages which lead to that desired centre of repose. My business in the City was too small to encourage my stay, my life there too sedentary to preserve my health, and the expense too big for my revenue, so that in obedience to your advice and my brother B's [John Bigge's] earnest invitation, I shall by this remove, remedy the first, promote the second and secure the last.

But while I am writing this, I receive yours of the 20th May; I am glad your lady is safely delivered and recovered from that dangerous distemper which ensued it: . . . methinks you multiply very fast, your first ability comes so fresh upon you, as if you had not only the power but the art of generation: others do it when they can, but you when you will; you do it by intention, they by chance. If you say 'let us make man', it is presently done, your fiat is immediately followed with a factum est. Like blades upon the road (if the expression be not too mean or misapplied) it is no more between you than 'stand and deliver'.

. . . Children are said to be blessings and money but a snare; the 'blessing' I have vigorously got, but the 'snare' I have vainly pursued. You may tell your lady that I fancy myself to be the representative of mankind, that I am employed by the public voice to congratulate her recovery and to thank her for obliging the living with such a bountiful increase. . . .

    Sir,

        your faithful servant,

            W.L.

LETTER 15

The succeeding years were unhappy ones. There was an increasing mutual hatred between Lawrence and his brother-in-law, John Bigge, which, with lack of employment and shortage of money, proved a disastrous combination. To occupy his time, Lawrence made a translation of Diego Saavedra Fajardo's *The Idea of a Prince Christian and Politick* and later made a study of Roman coins which had been collected and left with him by Isaac. Of the coins, he wrote that he made it 'not only my Diversion but my Study to discover the meaning of the Reverses and unriddle all their Historical Secrets'.

The household at Haines Hill consisted of John Bigge (of whom Lawrence wrote, his chief qualities were 'incivility, inhumanity, treachery'); his wife, Catherine (Anne's sister), and their children; John's younger brother, Richard (sometime parson, sometime doctor – apparently a gullible and foolish man and '. . . one of the smallest characters in the book of Nature; . . . you can hardly distinguish the creature, whether he be Man or Monkey, without the aid of a Microscope'); Anne's grandmother (of whom Lawrence was seemingly fond); Lawrence, Anne and Willy. Isaac, apparently, 'often wondered how I could waste my time under the roof of such a sordid mind, and associate myself with a temper so sullen and morose'. Lawrence explains that he did 'for the sake of the sisters wink at those things which I thought it had not been possible for me to see without visible contempt.' (*Diary*).

In this letter, again to Robert Fielding, Lawrence is returning to this unhappy domesticity after a visit to Shurdington.

LETTER 15

For Dr Robert Fielding   [Undated. 1670–75]

Sir,
Fortune who still feeds me with empty hopes and a [illegible in the manuscript] reversion, who upon the bargain of marriage gave me the earnest of many acres, but detains the possession of more, hath brought me back again to my old station. When I was retiring from Sherington and Gloucester I fancied my content (which is the blessing and beauty of life) to resemble that month wherein I left 'um; like the leaf upon the retreat of sap, it lost its nourishment, was shrewdly shaken, withered and decayed. I grew cold without and within. I had October beating on my face and beating at my heart. When I parted with those places, I parted with two real delights; in the former I took pleasure for my own sake, in the latter for yours; in the one I had the promised earth in prospect and in the other a friend in possession.

And were it not for those two, I mean my wife and my son, who are parts of myself, I might truly say, I am returned again to Egypt and spend my days in bondage. . . .

LETTER 16

INTRODUCTION

During his reign, Charles II called in and revised many city and town Charters (setting out their rights and privileges) mostly in an attempt to gain officials sympathetic to the Crown. The following letter is in response to a letter from Dr Robert Fielding on the subject.

Lawrence again criticizes the King, partly for the Stuart belief in the 'divine right of Kings'. Of his irreverent description of the animals at Court (the King also had a monkey which jumped on the Queen's lap, causing her to miscarry, and a talking starling) perhaps, as he wrote on a similar subject (letter 12) 'here is room enough for all the Whips of a Satirist'.

LETTER 16

For Dr Robert Fielding[25]   [Undated. 1670]

Sir,

. . . methinks letters from others taste of diversion and look like the issue of idleness or ease; but either as a physician or a magistrate you are so bound to a double care that your repose is not fixed to a saint's day or a dominical letter; you have always a pen in your hand or a spur on your heel, and the whole calendar is to you of an equal complexion. And therefore when you write, your kind intention makes a breach in your business, and so that which from another would be but a letter, from you is an obligation.

You tell me that your city is still divided and that you expect a hearing before the Privy Council.[26] I wish you success, but much doubt it for, in your case, the design is plain and you must lose your Charter to make way for greater things. Princes love to have the bridle in their own hands; they either believe or are flattered into an opinion that dominion is so theirs by divine right that they are to rule at pleasure, and their commands, right or wrong, are to be obeyed, not disputed.

---

25 Robert Fielding was not only a 'Dr of Phissicke' and a magistrate but an alderman of the City of Gloucester from 1662–71 and Mayor in 1664. In 1662 he had been one of the Commissioners appointed to administer the oath of loyalty to the Crown and the Church of England, required by the 'Act for the well-governing and regulating of Corporations' of December 1661.

(Bristol and Gloucestershire Archaeological Society, *Transactions* 1936, Vol. MLVIII)

26 The division in the City in 1670, leading to 'Disorders and Irregularitys', was over the election of a new Mayor. The Charter was declared forfeited in November 1671 on the grounds that failure to elect a Mayor, that year, was in breach of the terms of the Charter. Future Mayors were to be nominated, not elected, when the new Charter was granted (in order to ensure that they would be favourable to the King when elections were held).

(*P.C. reg* 63, Nov. 3 1671)

When you come thither you may perhaps think as I did, that is, if some brutes are endued with a kind of reason (which is urged and owned by many) and such a reason that may be improved by observation, then the royal spaniels may become knowing in the affairs of State; for they are always lying upon the table and made acquainted with the most secret debates. The dogs and the ducks are a happy race of animals, both of them much esteemed and daily fed by the King's own hand: and reason good; for the dog loves and fears; the duck swives and tipples: the Spaniel represents an obedient subject; and the life of a duck is the life of a King. These are the intrigues and the mean delights of a crown, though methinks Gods should busy themselves about sublimer things.

However it would be much better to make use of their power against those that slight it, and not against those that gave it: I mean, it is much more heroic to follow the warlike genius of their people and rather endeavour to conquer other nations, than enslave their own. King James the weak and the wise began it, but that our King may enjoy his rights, and the subjects vigorously defend their own is, I think, but the just wish of

Sir,

your faithful servant

W.L.

'methinks Gods should busy themselves about
sublimer things'

LETTER 17

INTRODUCTION

In 1672, the King had again declared war against the United Netherlands – this time in alliance with France – but without the consent of Parliament. Peace was concluded in March 1674 but not before Lawrence's brother, Isaac, had been caught up in the hostilities at St Helena.

Isaac, still trying to restore the family's 'ancient splendour', by repairing its fortunes, had decided to trade in India. The East India Company claimed a monopoly of trade in the East Indies so that, in order to avoid detection as an 'interloper', Isaac had set sail in a naval escort ship while his baggage travelled in an East-Indiaman. Unknown at home, the Dutch had captured St Helena and, although retaken by the Fleet, Isaac had been forced to return to England, while his possessions travelled on to India. (The incident is described in the *Dictionary of National Biography* – Sir Richard Munden – and in the *Diary*.) Isaac has been rewarded by the King and the East India Company for his part in recapturing the island, but needs further funds to renew his journey.

Lawrence writes to his uncle, to second his brother's request for financial assistance – a letter that would seem to have had the hoped-for result. Certainly Isaac sailed again for India in 1675.

Lawrence's letters to his uncle are often ponderous, which may say something of his uncle's personality – but more, perhaps, of their relationship.

LETTER 17

For my Uncle Wm. Lawrence Esq;   1675

Sir,

The late accident at St. Helena (which made our merchant a Man of War, and by dividing my brother from his effects brought him back to England and drove them forward to the Indies,) did not only surprise but might well discourage him from any future attempt. Yet he resolves to renew it, and by great promises here and great friends there, seems assured of a successful voyage. But yet, not knowing the fate of his adventure [investment], he thinks the present of 250 Guineas made him by the King and the Company not to be a sufficient foundation, and therefore I second the request he made to you, that you would be pleased to double the sum. But yet not (as was once desired) by way of payment but by way of gift. I know the former could not stir your reason, but I guess this latter will move your generosity.

As I have seen a gamester at Hazard (and he that trades upon the giddy element doth something resemble that person and that play) when he loseth he sets deeper, and at last at one throw recovers what he had lost at many. Between curiosity and commerce my brother hath parted with much time and treasure, gone many voyages [this was his fifth] and lost many sums, but makes one industrious push for all. He was not born under a lazy planet, he is willing to put both nature and fortune upon one throw, and at one stake to hazard both his estate and his person. Nor doth he thus expose himself for his own single interest, the main reason which tempts him to search after the treasures of the East, is, that in me or my son he may repair the ruins and raise your family to its ancient splendour.

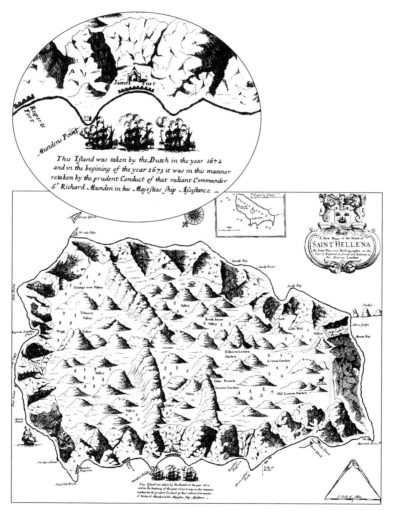

The island of St Helena
From *The English Pilot*, 3rd book, John Thornton, London 1703

He is eager to be gone, but without your assistance[27] he cannot well weigh anchor; it is your breath that must help fill the sails, and launch him into the ocean. . . .

Besides, Sir, what you formerly gave, though it be at a distance is still floating, and therefore in a new gift you will have this satisfaction, you may call it rather an addition than a supply. Had I my late ability, I would have prevented his request, but the blessed City of London was my horseleech and sucked away that which hath a proverbial comparison to blood; I thought it would only have breached a vein, but it pricked an artery, and had I not hastened away, I had quickly bled myself into cramps and convulsions.

Sir, in what I have writ, I do but intimate, not persuade; for your unerring judgment is easy to discern and quick to resolve; so that when I have said what I can, I must say one thing more, which is, that you have always made your own reason the primum mobile, and your liberality is seldom set in motion by any other wheels; yet in thus promoting my brother's request, I hope I have not too much strained those dutiful respects which have been so long and so nicely the care, that they are become the only concern of Sir,

your most obedient

W.L.

---

27 The ship in which Isaac had sailed as far as St Helena was the *Assistance*. (*DNB*: Sir Richard Munden.) She was 510 tons, a fourth-rater, with a crew of 100–150 men, and carried 34 guns. She had been built at Deptford in 1650.

LETTER 18

INTRODUCTION

The following sections from a long letter written to Isaac, after he left for India, cover the months of March–September 1675. In March, Lawrence is at Hurst, followed by a month at Shurdington, in April. If life with the Bigges is 'Egypt' and a life of 'bondage', so Shurdington is 'my little Canaan'.

John Bigge had given the Lawrences notice to quit Haines Hill and Lawrence hoped to persuade his uncle to allow him to bring Anne and Willy to live at Shurdington. He was doomed to disappointment but, returning to Hurst, found that he and Anne had been offered a refuge with neighbours, Sir Richard and Lady Harrison, at Hurst Place. The last sections of this letter, in resilient mood, are written from his new home.

The brothers are very close and Lawrence's enjoyment in setting out to 'divert' Isaac is evident. The latter is given family news – often of illness – which Lawrence usually describes in terms of a military siege, either withstood or in the capitulation of death.

The complete, much longer, letter forms one of the two main parts of the first, *Diary*, manuscript of Lawrence's writings. The extracts given here are in the 19th-century copy of the letters, in the possession of the editor.

LETTER 18

[To Isaac Lawrence]   [March–September 1675]

That the severe decrees of Heaven have again contradicted the requests of nature and not only designed another separation, but removed you into a more distant and a more dangerous clime, is a misfortune, which though I may frequently, yet methinks I can never sufficiently deplore. . . . I need not repeat how sad was my parting and how entire my love, lest in the former I might seem to suppose my society and in the latter my affection suspected. My last letter showed my own melancholy, but by this I will endeavour to divert yours, and give you a lepid [pleasant] account of things and persons.

MARCH

. . . And now comes the news of the death of my old Lady Grizel[28] and of the young Lady Elizabeth, this only peeped into the world and having seen her

---

28 Lady Grizel Lawrence, mother-in-law of Lawrence's younger uncle, Isaac, who had married his cousin (also Grizel – see family tree on p. xii).

founder, took a dislike at the object, so cried and died;[29] the other so old as if she had been exempted from Eve's fall and had a patent for eternity. She died in her sleep, and had not Death judiciously taken her napping, she might have baffled all his artillery of diseases and her tough constitution would have resisted the battery and held him play for many ages, which made me often think that when ever she should be inclined to travel towards Heaven, it must be after the manner of the prophet, not by death, but translation. But by this sudden surprise we may see that fraud is sometimes better than force; for the bulwarks without and her heart (that strong castle) within yielded at last to secret practice, which had never been subdued by open force; that which could not be battered, was at last undermined.

My Lady Grizel, my Grannam,[30] and my uncle seemed to have entered into a Triple League for the security of the body natural, as of late Spain, the States, and our King did for the safety of the Body Politic;[31] but my Lady by this surprise (as our King by the contrivance of the French), being forced to forsake the confederacy, hath left the other two to struggle for their liberties. My Grannam with her staff is always sitting and lies upon her guard that way, my uncle is always walking and shifting from place to place; so that if Death should come to the house it would be a hard matter to find him within. Whenever he thinks it convenient to withdraw, this epitaph may be well revived upon his tomb: Deffessus sum ambulando [I am weary with walking]. For he thinks that life depends so much upon the benefit of motion, that he never sits still, insomuch that I verily believe that his body turns in his bed like flesh upon a spit, and that his very rest is but like the sleeping of a town-top [communal spinning-top].

APRIL

I am now got to Sherington in the pursuit of more acres. What a temptation there is in earth! every one endeavours to lay such fast hold upon that element as if they never designed to leave it. Alexander, who thought many worlds to be but like little points and too small for the great circumference of his mind, found six foot of earth or a narrow urn wide enough for his body. He to gain empire visited those Indies by land, which you to gain wealth

---

29 Lawrence may mean 'the young lady' (small 'l') Elizabeth. His sister, Jane Hudson, had a daughter, Elizabeth, who died in infancy. Lawrence accused the child's father of 'foul dealing' in some transaction with Isaac – which would account for his saying the infant took a dislike to her founder.
30 Anne's grandmother, who lived with them at Haines Hill.
31 In fact, the Triple Alliance was between the three protestant States of England, the United Netherlands and Sweden, signed in 1668 (although a later 'concert' bound England and the United Netherlands to assist Spain if attacked by France).

visit by sea: he returned with safety and success: so I beseech Heaven that you may do the like; and if my prayer take effect, I will then say with Lucan, Jam nihil O superi querimur [now I have no complaint, O Gods].[32] But to leave this digression . . . [Lawrence writes of land which he is trying to acquire, which adjoins Shurdington and for which his uncle will pay].

Thus I tire my thoughts with the hopes of earthly acquisitions, and yet in the midst of these fancies I cannot but tax myself with vanity, and must needs cry out, O quantum est in rebus inane! [how great is the vanity of the world!][33] for since the pippin eaters of Paradise brought in mortality, there is nothing worth the sweat of our brow, for we are no sooner warm in the possession, but death finds his cold summons and thrusts us out of this life either by age or accident: or else it will in time shift into other families and that which was too much our care will be transferred and become the right of another; so that in one sense the opinion of Copernicus held true, for this sort of earth is constantly moving and, like the sports of Vulcan used by the Greeks with burning torches, is always shifting possession, and hastily passing from one hand into another; till at last, like those smaller lights, all must be wasted and consumed by a more wide and universal flame. . . .[34]

APRIL

And now you may imagine you see me climbing the hill, [behind the house] and as I go, I cannot choose but turn my eyes upon my little Canaan. I have been almost forty years wandering in the wilderness of this world, and yet know not when I shall reach the land of promise. I must be tossed about from place to place, like a ship from billow to billow, and must look for no rest, till I can with my living cargo, my wife and Willy, arrive in that long-expected port, and ride securely within the command of Sed-Castle.[35] For at present my uncle's house is like Alexander's horse, and cannot be brought to the reception of any more than himself, for having by choice and custom long used and as long delighted in retirement, he is very wisely unwilling in his latter days to increase the noise and business of his family.[36]

But now I am got to the top of the hill, I love the prospect so well, that I will not leave it, till I have told you what I can at one look discover. I see the

32 Lucan, *Civil War* 1.37.
33 Persius, *Satires* 1.1.
34 At the celebration of Hephaestia (Hephaeston was the Greek Vulcan) a relay torch-race was run. Plato *Laws* 776b and Lucretius 2.79 liken such a race to the transfer of life from one generation to the next.
35 Alias Shurdington, Little Sherington or Sherinton Parva. (In his Will, Lawrence describes himself of 'Sherington or Sedcastle'.)
36 This was the time when, having been ordered out of the Bigge household, Lawrence was seeking a home at Shurdington.

three divisions of the County, the Cotswold Hills, the Vale, and the Forest; the first eminent for pleasure, the second for profit, and the third for strength. On the Cotswold I see rich fleeces, delicate springs, places fit for all country diversion, and the head of the best-natured river in the world, the Thames; which fills itself at seven springs, contrary to the Nile, which empties itself at seven mouths; septem ossia Nili. In the vale, I see in a full stream the second English river, but of Welsh extraction, the Severn; she glides through many rich meadows bordered with fruitful cornfields and enclosed pastures, visible near 50 miles, and on her banks are seated and in sight, Worcester, Tewkesbury, and the pleasant city of Gloucester. And on the other side lies the Forest of Dean, famous for its excellent oak (the best in the world for shipping), and its many mines of iron, of which are cast guns and bullets; so that it at once provides both castles and artillery, and not only promotes our trade, but defends our seas. In a word, I can at one view discover from hence all things that are necessary for man, and many that are superfluous, or, (in the words of Camden) whatever can be required for life or luxury. . . .

AUGUST

The tragic scene of death is not yet finished,[37] there is one more that must make his entry and his exit; and that is our voluminous Cousin T.E.; he, who (when you were at Tytherington) having tired his invention with many healths, drank a full glass to the rising moon, being much concerned at her pale face, which he would needs have to proceed from sickness or sobriety; and not to be cured, but by a brimmer of claret; which he held up expecting the man in her middle should have reached forth his hand and pledged him; which not being done, he called him a pale-faced knave, bid her throw him from her circle, swore he had known him for a decayed vintner, and that when he broke, he ran thither with his bush,[38] thinking to have set up a tavern in that new world. But now the bitter cup of death hath spoiled the relish of all his other tipple, and his wishes are at rest, which in this world were but three: ale, more ale, and ale enough.

But how these three mighty bodies will pass the Stygian ferry[39] is a new question, for sure Charon will not be contented with a common naulam, but

---

37 Lawrence's brother-in-law, Robert Hudson (his sister, Jane's husband) had died unexpectedly in July. Death had also 'resolved to make a lusty banquet' and 'culled two more of the same size: my Cousin W., a very plump divine . . . and his laborious curate. . . . '.
38 An ivy-bush (sacred to Bacchus) was the common sign on taverns to show they served wine.
39 The ancient Greeks put a coin (naulam) in the hand or mouth of their dead to pay the ferryman, Charon, when crossing the Styx to the Elysian Fields.

'our voluminous cousin T.E.'

will require treble freight; for without much caution or a calm, their weight may endanger the ferryman and overset his boat. My cousin T.L.'s daughter died likewise about this time;[40] any one of the three may carry her under his arm into the other world, and it will look no otherwise than a liver or a gizzard trussed up under the wing of a turkey. . . .

I am now got to Bednall [Bethnal] Green, and am entered into the house of mourning [for his brother-in-law, Robert Hudson]; where I find my sister so much frighted and afflicted at her sudden loss that she soon miscarried.

The funeral was after this manner. The hall and parlour were hung with black cloth and escutcheons, there were about a hundred persons invited by tickets and rings given.[41] The body was carried to the hearse and the pall supported by Sir Thomas Allen,[42] Sir John Bendish, Alderman How, Alderman Dashwood, Capt. Cole and Capt. Bonnele, the hearse was adorned with escutcheons and attended by a train of 32 coaches to Stepney church, and there he was interred. The earth was so thronged with coffins,

40 Possibly Sir Thomas Lawrence (the recipient of letter 51 and the grandson of old Lady Grizel, who died in March).
41 It was the custom to send out invitations to funerals and to give mourning rings either before, or at, the service.
42 Possibly Sir Thomas Alleyn, Bt. an ex-Lord Mayor of London or possibly Captain Sir Thomas Allin, a distinguished naval commander, both of whom were known to the Lawrence family.

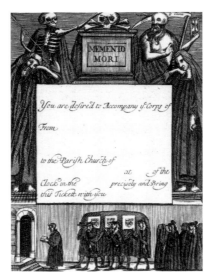

'*There were about a hundred persons
invited by tickets and rings given.*'
Funeral invitation ticket

that they were fain to take up his two little predecessors, Robert and
Elizabeth, and lay 'um upon him.

After this sad ceremony was passed I went to visit our old friend and
acquaintance Mr G.H. at Hackney.[43] Every Sunday morning from eight till
nine there is a sermon in his hall, and though perhaps neither the practice
nor the place may be unknown to you, yet it shall not slip without a
description. He very kindly invited me thither to a religious breakfast, but
my stomach was not acquainted with such early hours; besides I never loved
set meals in a morning, but was always for a bit and away.

But in the afternoon I went to take a view of his hall of prayer; which
indeed might pass for a church wanting nothing to that name but
consecration and a font; which latter I advised him to procure, though it
were but a kettle of cold water hung upon a pair of homely pot-hooks: for it
is a greater act of religion to make a Christian, than to instruct one. The first
thing I looked upon was two table[t]s hanging against the screen well
furnished with ten Commandments, a sort of meat very wholesome but of
hard digestion: and indeed like standing dishes at a feast, they are to be kept,
not eaten. The next is a great marble table, placed there for temporal food
when a long exercise had raised the appetite. It is cold enough to turn zeal

43 Probably George Hockenhull, a merchant who, with William Lawrence, senior, stood surety
for Isaac on his appointment as Factor at Surat for the East India Company in 1678 (*Diary*).

into an ague; and having been formerly broken, it might perhaps be set there as the emblem of a penitent, or stony heart broken by contrition. Then there stands a fashionable pulpit with a cushion to secure the elbow and the pious knuckle; and over all, the King's arms, with Honi soit qui mal y pense; but I know not whether it be designed for the King's Motto or their own. On the left hand aloft stands a suit of armour cap a pe [complete], to show perhaps, that this is not the Church triumphant but the Church militant; and it would be happy for the congregation if their pulpit could be always furnished with as sound a headpiece. Opposite to this is a gallery where his zealous wife sits with a train of young saints, all of them fitted with pen, ink and paper, ready to catch up the parson's words as they drop from his nose, and which having a holy twang are too precious to be lost.

At the top of this hall is a lantern and over that a vane: the former put me in mind of the many new lights that are started up in religion: the latter made me consider how apt the minds of men are to be turned with every breath, and to subject their very souls to the government of every giddy fancy: the vane of their religion turns with every wind of doctrine, so that I dare say there are as many sects and separations in the English church as there are points in the compass. The unsettled zealots, (who like the ignes fatui, generantur ex pingui et crasso, [foolish fires, produced from dense and thick (air)], and who fullness of bread and weakness of brain have made wanton in religion) greedily catch at any thing that is new and forbidden, insomuch that if there start up a meteor they presently gaze upon the new light, and follow it too, neither questioning its reality nor its conduct; so that I fear the Church of England thus crucified between the Papist and the many-headed Puritan, is but short-lived: these are the two thieves that endeavour to rob it of its glory, though the latter must needs be crushed in its fall, and surrender all to the undermining Roman Catholic as to the more working, powerful, and politic head.

But if I preach longer you'll go near to vote me into his pulpit and think me a fit man to recover lost sheep: and therefore I will leave this discourse and enter upon new matter.

AUGUST

When I went the next day to London I met with a thing like a charcoal thoroughly lighted at one end: for though his body was in black (picea caligine tectum) [covered in pitchy darkness][44] yet his face shone like a meteor: his countenance out-stripped Mr H. his hall and discovered a constellation, a whole assembly of new lights. His face (as you have seen) burnt blue again, like fire in a frost, or like a steel case to a watch set with

---

44 Ovid, *Metamorphoses* 2.233.

gold studs. If he peeps out of his window in a dark night, his lodgings are presently beset with engines and church buckets. I suppose by this time your expectation is upon the tenter to know the man: why, 'tis that glowing divine, that religious firebrand, who used to be at Mrs Hind's, whose face in an evening, especially when burnished with sack or brandy used to shine like a glow-worm. When I first saw him moving towards me at a distance, my thoughts were startled and I could not tell what to make of the apparition: sometimes I thought the sheriff was coming to make execution by a living Fieri Facias;[45] and sometimes that Diogenes had quitted his tomb and was walking about again with his dark lantern,[46] but when he came nearer I thought the dog-star itself had descended; for what with the extreme heat of the weather and this prodigious inflammation, I fell into a great sweat, and was scarce able to stay so long as to ask him how he did. I talked to him with my hand before my eyes, as children by a bongrace [brimmed hat] defend themselves against the heat of the sun; and indeed the fire was so great, that I was going to desire him to put out his face. But, thought I, if I should stir up his anger, God knows what mischief might be done by that additional heat; and so we parted.

[There is a post-script to the story of the fiery-faced parson in the *Diary* – written 4 years later]:

When I was at London I enquired after your old landlady Mrs Hind, and heard that she was married to the fiery parson, . . . and that she and her spouse were gone to live at Dover. Either his rectory lies there, or perhaps the King hath assigned him that post, that if he sees any danger at sea, he may give notice of it by turning his face towards the land; for it is always lighted, burns like a beacon and will give warning at as great a distance. . . .

SEPTEMBER

The gazettes will inform you that Turenne is slain by a great shot, and his Army, with much slaughter, forced over the Rhine.[47] That Crequis going to the relief of Trêves is totally routed. That the Prince of Condé, who after

45 A Sheriff's authority for executing judgement. Lawrence is, of course, making a pun on the parson's 'fiery face'.
46 The Cynic philosopher, Diogenes (he who lived in a tub), once set forth with a lantern, in the light of day, to search for a 'human being'. (Diogenes Laertius 6.41)
47 After peace had been signed between England and the United Netherlands in 1674, France had continued the war. Turenne and Condé were two of the three ablest of the French generals. The third, the Duc de Luxembourg, took over after Turenne's death and Condé's retirement the same year. Despite the setbacks Lawrence describes here, France made considerable gains the length of her eastern frontiers when the peace (of Nijmegen) was signed three years later.

Turenne's death took upon him the care of the Army, was shrewdly shaken, and forced to a hasty if not a shameful retreat. So the fortune of the French seems now to stagger, and that rash Monarch may live to repent, having ruined many towns and families, and shed much blood upon no other reason than to gratify his vainglory and ambition. . . .

Thus, my dear brother, I have finished this annal, and believe you will take as much pleasure in the perusing as I had in the penning. I could now in the close of this variety of matter enter upon a new theme and make our separation the subject of many lines; but it grows very late, and I must send away my packet tomorrow; yet though the night wears away apace and my dying candle draws near its end, my affection can never diminish or find a period, it can neither die nor consume, but will always burn with a steady and eternal flame in the heart of

Your truly affectionate brother

And faithful friend,

W.L.

'If he peeps out of his windows in a dark night, his lodgings
are presently beset with engines and church buckets'

LETTER 19

INTRODUCTION

Happily settled in his new home, Lawrence writes to his host, Sir Richard Harrison, who is staying in Wales. Sir Richard, an ex-royalist, was a Deputy Lieutenant of Berkshire.

Lawrence writes with gentle humour of the death of another neighbour, a keen fisherman, and then turns to the subject of the succession to the throne – the cause of some of the bitterest debate of Charles II's reign. The Queen, Catherine of Braganza, had failed to produce an heir and the heir-presumptive, James, Duke of York, as a self-confessed Roman Catholic, was unacceptable to most in the Country. Lawrence voices the popular fear that the King's confirmation of the illegitimacy of his eldest son, the Duke of Monmouth, could (by denying the possibility of an alternative, protestant, heir) lead to a Catholic uprising against the King and to enthrone the Duke of York.

LETTER 19

For Sir Richard Harrison
(at Coid-more in Wales)[48]   [Undated. March 1678/9]

Sir,

I am told by my Lady [Harrison] that you long for nothing more than to hear from me, and therefore I take the opportunity of this messenger to acquaint you that I am sorry I have so long forgot myself and you. I have no small share in the news of your safety, but my satisfaction would be higher, if the world were fruitful of accidents, and could furnish me with a journal of memorable things, whether acted on your own, or on a wider stage. I should be proud and pleased to divert your perhaps tired thoughts; and if I can waste some of your solitary minutes, I shall think I both honour and improve my own.

The air of Hurst grew moist upon your departure, and hath remembered your absence in many great showers; while you like the ark, was moving about the tops of the mountains, your lands have felt a little deluge, and yet lie covered with the flood: so that the Moors have not in all places an equal success, at Tangier they conquer, at Hurst they are overcome . . .[49]

---

48 Coedmore (near Cilgerran, Cardigan) was the estate of Sir Richard Harrison's orphaned grandson and ward, John Lewes, who spent most of his childhood with the Harrisons at Hurst. (Sir Richard's daughter, Catherine, had married the son of Colonel James Lewes of Coedmore – a royalist officer who had, perhaps, been a Civil War comrade of Sir Richard.)

(*The Lewes family of Abernantbychan*, David Huws, National Library of Wales)

49 A pun on the heathland of Hurst and the Moors who attacked Tangier. Tangier was part of Queen Catherine's dowry. It needed a garrison of 2000 men to protect it, at an annual cost of £70,000 and, after failing to sell it either to Louis XIV or the Portuguese, it was abandoned to the Moors in 1682.

'At Tangier [the Moors] conquer'
Tangier by Hendrik Danckerts

Sir T.H. after many removes from lodging to lodging is at last fixed, and hath taken a long lease in a narrower tenement: now the great angler is caught, the innocent fish may swim more securely in that element which was originally designed for their proper use and protection. The Kennet and the Lodden [local rivers] will be so sensible of their many and daily losses, that I believe the nymphs of those great rivers will hardly join with the mourners or shed one drop at the funeral. His baits and his hooks are now all at rest, and his line of life ends in another and a much longer line. So that you are become the last spark in the paper: like the morning star you have seen all the rest obscured, and beheld the exit of all the companions of your youth.

The Duke of Y. insinuates too fast; the King's power and politics are strangely fettered, for swayed by a working and perhaps a fatal faction he hath openly declared in Council that the Duke of Monmouth is his natural son:[50] a thing generally disliked not only because he is a protestant Prince of much courage and noble aspect; but because the way to the Crown being now more easy, the King's life is less secure. For all this while, the priests and Jesuits like so many moles work under ground and prepare for some great revolution. We blindly labour to settle the temporal succession, but how shall our religion continue in the right line and be defended from the spurious invaders? It is therefore the better policy because it is the greater piety, first to secure the Church and then the State.

But, Sir, my paper begins to swell like a spring tide; like the Lodden it overflows its just limits and may bring more damage than delight: while I designed to show those respects which by a long civility you have raised

---

50 The declaration, on 3rd March, had been made at the insistence of the Duke of York and was the price he exacted for agreeing to leave the Country at this time. (PC Reg. 67, March 3, 1678/9.)

'*A protestant Prince of much courage and noble aspect*'
James Scott, Duke of Monmouth and Buchleuch, after Kneller.

Sir Richard Harrison's monument by William Stanton in the
church of St Nicholas, Hurst.

and rivetted fast to you, I doubt I have tired your patience; especially since I do but actum agere [do that which is (already) done] and deliver those things, which I presume are more exactly drawn by another hand.

But by this time I suppose you are thinking of your return, are willing to leave the mountainous race of Brute,[51] and descend into a more fruitful soil: and therefore that the other half of your journey may be more speedily finished, and the other half of your person once more happily united, is the very serious wish of

Sir,

your faithful Servant

W.L.

51 Brut, or Brute, great-grandson of Aenaeus, was the mythological first King of the Britains (and after whom they were named).

LETTER 20

INTRODUCTION

Willy has been ill and Lawrence is aware of his vulnerability in having only one
link between himself and posterity – a vulnerability that introduces a new note
of tenderness in the character of the tetchy young man of the early letters.

LETTER 20

To Dr Robert Fielding   [Undated]

Sir,

Post varios casus [after various calamities], after many a storm and many a
doubtful symptom, tendimus [we arrive] in Latium.[52] Our small vessel sails
apace into the haven of health. My little Trojan, my one and all, hath for one
whole month struggled with a sharp distemper. A fever and an ague hath
pulled off his upper garments, I mean his flesh; and had sunk his spirits so
low, that both his limbs and his lungs grew very weak, and though they
continued life, yet they could hardly preserve motion. But now this dark
cloud breaks away, all things look serene again, and our little chick begins to
pick up his crumbs.

When our felicity hangs but upon one only thread, how the heart pants
and how fierce are our fears: he who had the dagger hung over his head by a
single hair had not a colder thought. . . .

---

52 Saturn lay hidden in Latium (in Italy) after he was driven out of Heaven by the Gods –
hence a place of refuge.

LETTER 21

INTRODUCTION

In May 1678, Isaac was desperately ill at Surat and, as he thought, dying. He wrote to Lawrence 'to take a last farewell of my dearest friend'. Nevertheless, he recovered within a few days and wrote that he was out of danger.

Lawrence seems to have had a telepathic knowledge of Isaac's illness and answered both letters:-

LETTER 21

September 20th 1678

Most dear Brother,

. . . I find that the will of heaven governs all, and that we can only reckon by our love and our wishes. It was the same night and hour (as near as I can guess) wherein you expected your dissolution and took leave of the world and me in those passionate and obliging lines, that I had this dream: methoughts my great desire to see you had landed me at Surat, where, thinking to have surprised you with an unexpected visit, I entered into your lodgings, but to my own greater surprise, I saw you wrapped up in your winding sheet, and lying pale, thin, and dead in your coffin. The horror of the object put me into such loud and bitter lamentations, that methoughts I reversed the decrees of fate and called you to life again. I waked and immediately with much disturbance but with little faith, related to my wife this sally of my fancy and the success of her long voyage.

Perhaps if a friendship can make such a perfect union, that one cannot suffer but the other must have some share in it. Or, if every man hath an angel (a being of the swiftest motion) to attend him. Or, if God's omniscience will sometimes oblige his creatures with a ray of his knowledge, then possibly by those we may understand the nearest, and by this the remotest concern. This dream of mine I do not look upon to be matter of chance, but an intimation from the divine favour, for I could never think that the soul could by any other means or at any other time arrive at an immediate knowledge of such distant actions. . . .

LETTER 22

After his recovery, Isaac was admitted into the East India Company but, a year later, had written that he was again ill.

LETTER 22

January 23rd 1680

Most dear Brother,
Your two letters of May the 23rd and May 30th via Aleppo, I have received this 23rd of January in the morning. I saw the superscription was writ by your hand, and so had little reason to doubt of your safety, but by what secret dictates of the mind I know not, my heart trembled and for many hours I could not break the seals, but when I had hovered thus till night, full of anxiety and disturbed thoughts, I at last opened the suspected paper, and read (but alas! with what little content) the contents of your letters. . . .

Among all the shocks of fortune nothing ever made me stagger so much; hitherto though my heels have been often in danger, I have still recovered and secured my footing; though some pills have been bitter, yet I have quickly met with some mild events which have soon washed away the unpleasing relish; I never yet heard of your danger or sickness, but at the same time I was also blessed with the news of your escape or recovery. But now providence brings me into a labyrinth and then takes away the clue; . . .

How long have I flattered myself that I should see you shine equal with the best of your friends; that you would increase in wealth and title, grow rich abroad and great at home! for so clear is my affection, that, provided you may have no cloud, I fear no eclipse, and could be proud in your fortune, though humble in my own. . . . But . . . while my wishes were passionately intent upon your fortune, I am now come even to despair of your life. . . .

Your much loving and much afflicted Brother,

W.L.

LETTER 23

In 1679, John Wright, M.P. for Ipswich, had written to Lawrence asking permission to marry his widowed sister, Jane Hudson. Now he writes both to give the news that the marriage has taken place – and that Lawrence's beloved brother, Isaac, after his further illness, has died at Isphahan in Persia. The depth of affection and understanding between the brothers leaves Lawrence devastated by his loss.

Without Isaac, there is also now little hope of the fortune on which the family's renewed lustre was to be founded. Isaac has died; Willy has been near death; but still William Lawrence, senior, now 86, lives on. At a time when property, particularly land-ownership, was the measure of a man's standing, Lawrence's inheritance is as elusive as ever. The desire for wealth, Lawrence once wrote to his uncle, 'if it regard the nobler ends, is certainly a most innocent ambition, and the highest mark of human prudence' (*Diary*).

As a member of Parliament, John Wright is involved in the developing crisis in the Country. King and Parliament had become increasingly out of step: the King was francophile, Parliament francophobe; rumours of a 'popish plot' against the King's life spread, and Parliament had passed the second of two Test Acts, excluding Roman Catholics from holding seats in Parliament, as well as from public office. In 1678, for the first time, there was open suggestion that the Roman Catholic James, Duke of York, should be debarred from the succession. This led to the crisis when, encouraged by the King's illness in August 1679 (when he was thought to be dying), attempts were made to exclude the Duke from the throne by Act of Parliament.

Hoping to gain a more sympathetic House of Commons, the King twice dissolved Parliament in 1679 (in January and again in July) and prorogued a further Parliament in October, which was not recalled for a further year. John Wright was re-elected to represent Ipswich in both elections – but, for Lawrence, the news of Isaac's death overshadows everything else.

LETTER 23

For John Wright M.P.   [Undated. *c*. February 1680]

Honoured Sir,

Your letter was an equal mixture of light and shade; one part seconds the report of my brother's death, the other confirms the news of my sister's marriage. I was sorry that this latter intelligence must be accompanied with so dark a cloud, and that the joy which was due to your nuptials must be sullied by so severe a fate. I ought to have made more haste to have congratulated you upon your new possession, but my brother's death shook me so rudely, that my soul seemed deprived of all its organs, and might be rather said to live than move; my affliction at so great a loss had disordered all my intellectuals, and left me either no thoughts to consider, or no leisure to reply.

But now the waters being a little assuaged, the ark opens, and I begin to look abroad. But to follow the method of your own letter which is indeed but the order of the creation, which says, that the evening and the morning were the first day, I cannot but show my dark side first; I cannot but tell you, that as my brother's great virtues and particular merit made every one deplore his hard fate, so his generous affection to me, visible by a long experience, cuts deeper and hath hewed down all the happiness of my life: for in him I saw the utmost limits of human goodness, and all the kind actions that nature or friendship could produce.

In which few words having drawn you, as it were in little, the picture of my grief, I will for the present lay by my night of sorrow, and welcome the morning, I mean, the news of your marriage; it being no small pleasure that you have revived the appellation of the dead and honoured me with the same title. I doubt not but every one hath saluted you with the common phrase of, I wish you joy, but because my knowledge of your choice may be either wider than theirs, or at least my content of a different size, I will change the expression, and only wish you both a long life; for considering her virtue and your merit, I need not wish you happiness, but only that you may long enjoy it; for I dare say, so long as you are sure of your life, you are sure of felicity; your blessings I conclude are certain, it is only life that is the bubble, which by a sad experience I see is easily, and in my brother was untimely broken.

I will say no more in the case but this, that you and your corporation have made a judicious election; they have chosen a good man for their burgess,[53] and you have chosen a good woman for your wife: but, if you will give me leave to thrust a lepid expression into a sad and serious reply, if you shall do no more in marriage, than you have lately and are likely to do in Parliament, you will make but few acts in that house, and but few children in your own.

But the remembrance of my brother's loss chides me for this excursion of fancy, it allows no cessation of grief, and shuts out all but sad and solitary thoughts. I wait to know the time of his death, that my sorrows may set apart a day to his memory and the contemplation of human frailty.[54] In the mean time I hasten to possess my new title and to assure you that I am

your very affectionate

Brother

W.L.

---

53 Members of Parliament were either Burgesses (representing Boroughs) or Knights of the Shire (representing Counties).
54 Isaac had, in fact, died on 10th August 1679 (his 40th birthday).

LETTER 24

INTRODUCTION

The fears induced by rumours of, in particular, the fabricated 'popish plot', to assassinate the King and enthrone the Duke of York, had reached fever-pitch in 1679. They added fuel to the efforts of those who wanted to exclude James from the succession. The 'Exclusion Crisis', the greatest test of Charles II's reign, lasted from the Spring of 1679 – when the House of Commons first introduced an Exclusion Bill – until March 1681. A second Bill was passed in the Commons in October 1680 but was rejected by the Lords.

The King had agreed to a formula limiting the powers of a Roman Catholic monarch, hoping it would be acceptable to the Exclusionists, but this was rejected. Instead he was pressed to divorce Queen Catherine, and remarry, to produce a legitimate Protestant heir. He refused. Considering his 'faultiness to her in other things', he said, it would be 'a horrid thing to abandon her'. The 'Williamites' favoured Prince William of Orange, married to James' protestant eldest daughter, Mary (a marriage the King had arranged three years earlier to appease the Protestants.) Others favoured the Duke of Monmouth (the eldest of the King's illegitimate children) – a suggestion the King rebutted with: 'much as I love him, I'd rather see him hanged'. The King was determined. The legal succession must be upheld or the Monarchy itself would be threatened.

Parliament felt confident of being able to compel the King to accept the Exclusion Bill by applying financial pressure – a method that had so often worked before. The King, however, used delaying tactics and, when a new Parliament was finally summoned in March 1681, it was on ground of his own choosing: Oxford had been a Royalist 'haven' since the Civil War.

LETTER 24

For John Wright Esq;   [February–March] 1680[1]
[Member of Parliament]

Sir,

A sedentary life, that is, sitting too long, being found very destructive to health, and the common parent of the gout and the stone, the royal care hath given you all leave to stretch your legs and visit your several Counties. But supposing you to be now ready to repair to your new seats and your old business, I send this letter to meet you half way, and to wish that by the King's making use of a quicker eye, and a gentler ear, much unity and more success may attend your next session.

Whenever you stand, you are in all respects a candidate, your election was never tainted with the bribe of the barrel, it comes always by pure choice, never by purchase.[55] But in these parts there hath been a great consumption of the liquid manufacture, and the taps have been all running after voices [votes]. It is a little hard that a man can't serve his Country without leave from the brewer, that the hoops must lead in the hollow, and the election must totally depend upon the choice of good liquors. So that in many places one may properly say that the merits of men are gauged; they are measured not by the brains but the barrel. He that draws most gallons shall have the most voices. A sad misfortune in a State: for how can we expect a blessing when debauchery must usher in our great debates, when our Senate must owe its being to liberal drinking, and that grave House must be built upon a cellar. A man of fancy might be apt to say, that while our members deal thus vigorously with beer and ale, it is easy to expect a disturbed head and staggering State.

We shall now see how the Oxford air will operate, and whether a nemine contradicente will shrink at the sight of a square cap, or be daunted at a flight of crows and magpies.[56] The great Y is almost jostled out of the alphabet, there is but one letter behind him, that is, the crooked Z, only hinders him from passing by; I mean the ill-contrived zeal of the pulpit keeps him from his third pilgrimage and won't let him go without much grumbling in the gizzard.[57] Though it seems to be with the people as it is with the letters, the numbers of the Excluders are at least two and twenty for one:[58] sufficient odds if it could be seconded by the Royal fiat.

I hope you will sit quietly, and effectually secure his sacred person, which must be by defending his 3 lions from the 3 lilies, and his 3 crowns[59] from the 3 mitres, that is by the ruin of popery and the French faction.

I will give you a visit at Oxford, if the session last any time, of which there seems to be no great assurance, for it is to begin in a blustering month, a month which participates as well of the lion as the lamb. And I the rather fear it, because I hear that Venus is still in the ascendant, and the ladies of pleasure are to attend his Majesty thither; and if so, then his seeming intentions will be very uncertain . . . [60]

---

55 Bribery, both of M.P.s by foreign governments to secure their interests and, in this case, of the electorate to secure their votes, had become standard practice. In the election of early 1681, the King had obtained money from Louis XIV to support his 'bribe of the barrel'.
56 i.e. the Exclusionists who may be daunted by the royalist dons and clergy of Oxford.
57 i.e. the 3rd attempt to pass the Bill excluding the Duke of York may finally succeed, despite the zeal of the clergy (and the voting power of the Bishops in the House of Lords).
58 At the election of 1681, the 'Excluders' returned to Parliament were more in the proportion of 3–1.
59 The Act of Union, uniting the three Kingdoms of England, Scotland and Ireland was not passed until 1707 – nearly 30 years later.
60 The King's French mistress, Louise de Kéroualle, Duchess of Portsmouth, and Nell Gwynn were in the entourage. (On reaching Oxford, Nell lent from her carriage and called 'Pray, good people, be civil. I am the Protestant whore!')

Sir, I heartily thank you for the very kind and passionate remembrance which you have of my brother's untimely fate; a loss that still shakes my very being, and is enough to drive me into a contempt of all human things. But that your remaining years may have a long extent and an easy period; and that we may live to see these rising storms of State gently expire and settle into a calm, is (I am sure) your common prayer as well as mine; they daily employ, but can never tire the devotion of,

Sir,

your affectionate Brother

W.L.

Charles II, bust by Honoré Pelle

POST-SCRIPT TO LETTER 24

Parliament met at Oxford in March. The King still tried for conciliation but it became obvious there could be none. The Commons passed a third Exclusion Bill – but they had not reckoned on the King's resolve. He would not, 'in honour, justice and conscience', agree to his brother's exclusion from the throne. A week after Parliament first sat, he went to the House of Lords (with his state robes travelling secretly in a sedan chair) and dissolved Parliament.

The tide of feeling in the Country had already begun to turn – and there was little reaction to the Exclusionists' defeat. The King obtained funds from King Louis XIV and from the increasing revenues from customs and excise, which allowed him to dispense with Parliament until his death four years later.

Titus Oates' 'Popish Plot' fabrication was almost universally believed – and encouraged by the extreme Exclusionists – in order to gain support from the voters to the Exclusion cause. The King, himself, gave no credence to the plots but was fearful of revolution. The terms 'Whig' and 'Tory' (Scots and Irish for 'outlaw' respectively – and both being named by their opponents) were first used during the Exclusion Crisis. Lawrence's support for the Exclusionists and his belief in limiting the prerogative powers of the Crown, show him to be a Whig, albeit moderate. He was no republican.

In the *Diary*, Lawrence gives one reason for the hysterical antipathy to Roman Catholicism. In the 1679 letter to Isaac, he writes of the Popish Plot: 'If the Papists get to the helm there may be expected in time a massacre or at least an extirpation of almost all the gentry, for the old revenues of the Church (whose detention in their judgment is sacrilege, and not to be allowed nor forgiven because a mortal sin) being dispersed into their hands, [i.e. since the dissolution of the monasteries] they must cut off all who can pretend a title and are able to make new Revolutions'. 'This conjecture,' he continues, 'is not to be despised, nor is it much to be feared in this Kingdom so long as there is unity and a joint opposition . . .'.

In the same letter, he wrote: 'The two things feared are the designs of the Papists and the power of the French'. (There was constant fear of a French invasion at the time, in support of the Roman Catholic cause.) Priests and, in particular, Jesuits were seen as agents of Louis XIV, working for the overthrow of the State. (In letter 19, Lawrence had described them as 'moles'.) It was a fear that led to the cruel excesses of the Popish Plot and Exclusion crises when many priests were tried and executed.

The Tory writer, Roger North (1653–1734) gave an opposing view. It was a time, he wrote, 'when wise men acted like stark fools . . . '.

LETTER 25

INTRODUCTION

William Lawrence, senior, has at last died – at the age of 88 – and Lawrence has inherited Shurdington, the home he has dreamed of for so long.

Lawrence's relationship with his uncle shows him in one of his less attractive lights. He owed his uncle all his advantages: William Lawrence had made him his heir, had paid for his education and made the settlement of money and property at the time of his marriage to Anne (of which he wrote to Isaac, 'I thought my everlasting Uncle would never have parted with any of his precious acres, but now the inheritance of the greatest part lies wrapped up in three great skins of parchment').

The *Diary* contains numerous letters written to William Lawrence, senior, at New Year and on the anniversary of Lawrence's marriage. They are fulsome in their gratitude and wishes for his uncle's health and happiness. Most are signed 'your obliged and grateful nephew' – as indeed they might be. At the same time he is writing to Isaac – in 1659, as we have seen, 'my uncle is not yet turned marble'; in 1667 (above), '. . . my everlasting uncle'; in 1679 that 'my Uncle is entering into his annus mirabilis – which is a prodigious heap of years, and looks as dreadful as the Spanish invasion'; in January 1680 (in a letter written to Isaac after the latter had, in fact, died) he writes: 'the numerous years of my Uncle, of which I may now with some justice complain, have stripped me of my happiness, robbed me of my best years, and crushed a mind which I once thought was designed for a much wider circle, than my life now enjoys or his death can give . . . '. To be fair to him, his honesty in recording these and other passages of which, in retrospect, he cannot have been proud, is admirable – nor, witness the 'Spanish invasion', is he always serious. The letter of 1667 continues: '. . . when he shall be willing to die, of which there is so little probability that I think it is left to his own election, the earth need not be opened for him, it will be sufficient to engrave an epitaph upon his body, and lay him down for his own monument; for I dare say, as he now outlives men, he will then out-last marble. But to leave jesting, he hath dealt nobly by me and as he hath received my thanks so he deserves my prayers for a much longer life; for his only intention of living single was, that in me he might repair the ruins of his family . . . '.

Lawrence is writing to a cousin in the Army. In the third Dutch War of 1672–4, the French Navy had fought under English command and the King's regiments had fought, as auxiliaries, under French command. When peace between England and the United Netherlands was signed in 1674, English soldiers continued to be used, and recruited, until war ended between France and the United Netherlands in 1678. The cousin to whom Lawrence is writing had, by inference, fought in this French Army. Now, for a short time there was peace, although Lawrence predicts, correctly, that this will not last. The following year France and Spain were at war in the Spanish Netherlands.

On a visit to Hurst, he writes of the election of their knight of the shire, but the rumour that the King intended to call an election was unfounded.

LETTER 25

For — [a cousin]   November 10th 1682

A long distance is the crime of fortune, but a long silence is the offence of the will; the former may be of a necessity and must be endured; but the latter is either from choice or neglect. You were much in my debt and even to a fault, but the two letters which you lately sent me, shall wipe off the chalk and make amends for all.

I am glad you have survived the various fortunes of the war, and have for some time enjoyed the delights of peace; though perhaps to you a storm is more pleasing than the active dangers of the field.

My little family is well, but my uncle weighed down with the burden of 88 years, is at last sunk into the earth: his life was not easily resigned, his heart was very strong, and tugged hard for a greater number.

But as to your other enquiry, the times are very still and afford little news; only in the County of Berks, where I now am, we have this one sign of an approaching Parliament: the jure-divino men and all the birds of the black feather begin to appear in flocks,[61] and solicit for voices. On Tuesday last the gentry were invited by the Mayor of Reading to a great feast; but very few appeared, though the Earl of Clarendon was there in person with his two royal arguments, a brace of fat does.[62] At this feast the circingles were much more numerous than the belts;[63] and it did not so much look like a meeting of the gentry, as an assembly of divines. But after dinner when these Black birds had drunk a few chirping cups and the wine had warmed their passive principles, it was moved and agreed, by a formal subscription, that Mr B. a rich brewer and a rank Tory, should be their Knight of the Shire. When they parted, the clergy looked like so many Cornish choughs, with black bodies and red bills, their faces being thoroughly lighted either with zeal or claret.

In this and other Counties the pulpits are generally hot and fiery; they are so very fond of power and so infected with pride and pluralities, that they care not how far nor how swift they run. They even shut their eyes upon natural reason, and shelter all their follies under an obstinate and blind obedience. The power and pride of the priests have ruled and ruined many kingdoms: and I dare say our clergy stick so close to the royal interest for no other reason than to promote or secure their own. If the King or the State should offer to clip their wings every levite [parson] would be a Thomas à

---

61 i.e. 'divine-right' men and the clergy – supporters of the Tory Party.
62 Henry Hyde, 2nd Earl of Clarendon. His sister, Anne, was the first wife of The Duke of York and he was, consequently, the uncle of the two princesses, and future Queens, Mary and Anne of York.
63 i.e. the clergy were more in evidence than the peerage.

Becket, the whole tribe would be contented to see the Crown bow to the mitre, and the great council strike sail to a convocation.[64]

The business of the world is nothing but intrigue and treachery, in both which you must not forget that the French King is the greatest example: his false heart observes no peace nor the oaths that bind it: what other princes win by an open courage he often gets by fraud or steals by surprise: his restless ambition will quickly beat the drums again, and you must not think to sleep long in a garrison.

And therefore if in this short interval of war you can give your friends a visit, you shall be to none more welcome than to

Your loving Cousin

W.L.

'a brace of fat does'
Princess Mary, later Queen Mary II, after Lely and Princess Ann, later Queen Anne,
after Wissing

---

64 The Church of England, which owed its continued existence to the Restoration, maintained its loyalty to the King, although its political power had been reduced. Lawrence frequently refers to 'levites' or the 'tribe of Levi' when writing of parsons – in this case inferring that the Church of England would like to regain greater political power.

LETTER 26

INTRODUCTION

Something of what it meant to have come into his inheritance is indicated by the next letter. No longer a guest in other people's houses, Lawrence is now a man of standing whose advice is sought by the neighbourhood. A Mr Grafton has consulted him on his proposed marriage. It is no surprise to find that Lawrence considers the widow's library to be not the least of her attractions.

Shurdington (the Greenway) c. 1910
The cupula, since removed, was designed as a study for Willy

LETTER 26

For Mr Samuel Grafton   August 15th 1684

Sir,

Your letter brings me a double obligation, first, that you lay open to me your private thoughts, and next, that you desire my advice in a matter of such weight and concern. If my wife hath been instrumental in proposing a way to increase your happiness, I shall think it no small addition to my own. As to the substance, which is marriage; I have of late years thought your life too lonely, and that a change of condition would much lighten that melancholy and divert those thoughts which are incident to a retired and single life. But as to this, you yourself are the ablest judge, and need only follow your own private opinion.

But as to the circumstances and the matter of your enquiry, that is, the qualities and fortune of the widow; in the former my experience is little; in the latter my knowledge is less. But this I can say, for ought I have observed myself or could ever hear from others, she is pious and prudent, careful in her house, calm in herself, and in her nature so very easy and obliging. That there needs no other character to recommend and make her fit for your choice. And though her beauty be gone with her youth, yet I suppose your wary judgement hath no strong fancy for such fading pleasure, provided that flaw were well covered by things more durable and solid.

Her husband was reputed to be very rich, and I believe he was so, but I know nothing of either the quantity of his estate or of the certainty of the report, having never had either the occasion or the curiosity to enquire. Let my wife ask, what her estate is and where it lies, and thereby open a way for your further search; that so you may have a sufficient invitation to woo, and full satisfaction before the tedious knot be tied.

Yet I verily believe if you can reach her, you will enter into a double treasure; one of much money, the other of much learning; for the volumes which were left her are very choice, many, and of great value so that if she were a little mended before, and her books gilded behind I think no man can have a better wife, and no house can have a nobler furniture. Besides there is one thing very considerable, I really believe she hath not the subtlety of many widows, who give away themselves but either conceal or detain their fortunes; bringing to the poor yokefellow a small store of money, and a great stock of repentance.

Sir, may you meet with much satisfaction and success in the pursuit of your little voluminous widow; may she be your totaliter, body and books. The book hath a cover but the widow wants one, and will therefore bind herself for life, and part with all her money, goods and liberty to purchase it.[65] But that you may be the only man destined to this happy bargain is both the hope and expectation of

Sir,

Your Friend and Servant

W.L.

---

65 Probably a pun, partly a ribald reflection of Lawrence's new familiarity with the farmyard and partly a reference to the legal term 'feme covert' (as opposed to 'feme sole') of a married woman.

LETTER 27

INTRODUCTION

Lawrence has come to his 'safe harbour' at last, but the tranquillity is shattered by Willy. He is an undergraduate at Oxford and has become engaged to the daughter of a local landowner, older than himself, and of whose father's intentions Lawrence is suspicious: Mr B. is attempting to disrupt the terms of the marriage settlement. It is a wise and forbearing letter to a son who is only eighteen – and on whom all his hopes for the future of the family are pinned.

Lawrence's content in being at Shurdington must also be lessened by Anne's being ill. Six years earlier, he had written to 'Madam Hanna Fielding' (whom he addresses as 'Cousin' and who is, presumably, the wife of Dr Robert Fielding) of 'my wife's long sickness and many severe sufferings which I cannot well describe, for no expression can be so acute as her pains'. In this letter, he again writes of her 'distemper' which suggests the illness was recurrent. But, for the moment, Willy's engagement is the most pressing of his concerns.

LETTER 27

For my beloved Son Mr Wm. Lawrence
at Trinity College

[Undated. 1686]

Dear Willy,

The late earnest desire that I would seal one part of the indentures of settlement, wherein I was to acknowledge satisfaction and own the receipt of a great sum, above two months before the designed time of payment, without any solid reason for so much haste or any offer either of a collateral of security, or a sight of that mortgage which was to make good the residue, hath alarmed me with a strong suspicion of the integrity of the persons and of the reality of the portion. But I will wait for the further evidence and have a special care that the trust be securely lodged, for upon a narrower inspection I see many reasons, why it cannot without apparent hazard be settled in R.B. in whom I perceive they have without my allowance reposed it, for which purpose I intend at the Assizes to propose my objections to some able lawyer, and am certain he must concur with my opinion; for if my shallow eyes can see so much, those who have a deeper insight into these affairs, and are enlightened by long practice can make a nicer enquiry.

In the mean time and to prepare you against any accident, I will muster up into one body those many inconveniences which I have passim but often urged and which will certainly attend this marriage; partly that while I sift the secrets of this trust I may discharge the higher trust of nature; and partly that you may not hereafter complain for want of caution.

I always advised you (as being my single and particular care) that you would not make too much haste to marriage, but first to take in learning and then love: and when discretion as well as nature had made you ripe for that condition, my advice was, that you would place your first aim at a good fortune, for plenty is the best thing to maintain a family, secure love, and expel cares. But here I doubt that when you shall come to open your house, you will find the revenue of £350 an: too straight, and though we should be very willing to add to your livelihood; yet by reason of your mother's distemper, I mean the great charge of seeking distant remedies and living in remote places, we may not be able to contract our own.

Your son will be ready to take before you have ability to give: and during our lives all your industry cannot rake up one single portion; and so, to the great reputation of the distaff and the needle, your house shall be filled with long coats and superannuated girls. You will fall into a fruitful race and a numerous family; the one will increase your cares, and the other your expense: for, by reason of the cohabitation, and the proximity of alliance, not only all their kindred, but all their acquaintance must be made yours. And if R.B. (being only tenant for life) should die before he can make a full provision for his children, their fortunes would be small and you may notably feel the inconvenience.

Consider your tender years, and your slender experience, the former not fit for, and the latter not acquainted with the business of the field. Your education (for which I have had a particular care) will be so absolutely lost, that your genius must be totally employed about the plough, the mow, and the cow; and you will never have brains enough to manage the common honours and business of your country. You must for three years sit at the lower part of the round table filled with women and children; and when R.B. is either weary or unwilling to entertain company, you must be the deputy and supply his office in all the drudgery of drinking. You must be the gentleman-usher to all visits received and given; an office hateful to the ingenious, as too effeminate, soft and slavish. And when you are once tied by the leg, you must be employed to flutter and entice more larks into these nets of marriage.

Add to this, that your wife will first come of age, and then, as the law gives her a priority in judgment, she may in reason aim at a priority in power: and indeed I easily foresee, that if your love shall not incline you to be obedient to her and her parents, you will be infallibly checked and slighted. Dum Spiro Spero [while there's life, there's hope] will be a useless motto; you will in one moment see the full extent of your hopes, and certainly much will be lopped away by their crossing your humour, and the pleasure of thinking, when you shall see the pillars erected and a ne plus ultra put to the growth of your fortune; for here the present portion is declared to be your utmost expectation, nor can you guess at any accident that may increase it.

You will see all the advantages and pleasures of youth lost in a narrow fortune, and overwhelmed in a heap of cares; and what may now be promoted by love, and a youthful heat, will certainly in a small time cool into melancholy and repentance; which may always afflict your mind, but can never recover the freedom of your life.

Willy Lawrence by Johann Kerseboom
painted *c.* 1691

And how can you be so strongly possessed with the opinion of their future kindness, who pinch you in small things and labour so hard to make you a bare tenant for life to almost my whole estate; whereby you would sell your birth-right to please your fancy, and for a trifle so lose the freedom of your life and fortune, that upon any extremity you could neither relieve yourself, command your heir, or prefer your children? Add to this that upon a full consideration of your great temperance, many great endowments of nature, and some of fortune, I have always thought you well qualified for the advance of your self and your family by a marriage; which latter I the rather desired, because in others it is frequent, but in ours it hath but twice happened in above 500 years:[66] and we daily see that those improvements which depend upon a bare frugality, are very laborious, slow, and uncertain.

But to conclude, . . . since love is blind in youth, and therefore wants the instruction of riper years to open and clear its eyes, I have now put you in mind of these things; but yet with this assurance, that if your resolution be stronger than my reasons, or if my money can be sure and the trust safe, I shall certainly proceed to a consummation; for in this case of a wife I pretend only to advise, not to choose; and only to direct your reason, not to divert your love. And indeed were it not in relation to the security and your particular case, there could be no exception in quality, person, or portion; but

66 The Lawrences traced their descent from Sir Robert Lawrence, who had been knighted at the battle of Ptolemais (Acre) by King Richard I in 1191.

as things are, I would present the lady with this verse in Ovid, changing the name only, Ex omnibus unum Elige, sana, virum: modo non sit in omnibus unus [From them all, select one, sensible woman, for your husband, only let not this one be among them].[67]

But as to the main matter weigh well what I write, for my suspicions have a solid foundation, and affairs of this binding nature require the most searching prudence; for we must not be so wrought upon by great pretences, and outward shows of kindness, as to commit any error that may leave us to repentance and an aftergame; the one being the torment of the judicious, and the other the remedy of fools.

When we are jealous of sands or concealed rocks, it is but high time to throw out the plummet or make use of some skilful pilot: and you yourself shall go with me to see the answer and advice that shall be given upon my queries: for to have you settled upon such a firm basis, as may not be subject to be shaken either by their act or our omission is the chief design of

My dear Willy, thy most affectionate

Father

W.L.

---

67 Ovid, *Metamorphoses* 10, 317–8 (the original has 'Myrrha' for 'sana' and 'dum ne' for 'modo non').

LETTER 28

INTRODUCTION

The lawyer, it seems, did his work well and Mr B. (Reginald Bray Esq;) did not like the terms of the contract – although Lawrence suggests that the final terms would have been generous. Perhaps there were two sides to the story: Willy had not, apparently, been guiltless. 'I wish,' Lawrence wrote to Mr Bray 'my son's addresses had been rewarded either with an earlier period or a smoother fate; but since his little, his very little errata's (by him not understood and to me unknown) have made so deep an impression on your mind, I am well satisfied to see the whole business brought to a conclusion.'

LETTER 28

For my beloved Son Mr Wm. Lawrence.
At Trinity College.   [Undated. 1686/7]

My dear Willy,
Great is my content at the assurance which you give me of your health, and of that discreet resolution which you have assumed to recover those many months by your diligence which you have so unhappily lost by your love. For this passion if it fall upon very young years, and be not well backed by sound reason and advantage, is but the appetitus concupiscilis, the bare heat of nature, and so levels you with the meanest part of the creation. But by searching into the works of the learned and laying up the treasures of knowledge, you rise to more generous things; you show a soul nobly extracted, and by refining your reason you more resemble that glorious Being that bestowed it.

Opportunities for learning have their critical times; they are bald behind,[68] and if they once retire, they return no more; but the markets are always full of females, you may choose at your leisure, for fair faces with fair fortunes are hic et ubique and are no miracles in this age. Daughters must marry when they can, but sons may marry when they please, and are not so much limited in time, having either less heat or more liberty.

You tell me they now talk as if I could not make good what I promised, but that which they publish there would here be derided. I knew the whole swarm of B.s were offended, and since they could not get you into their hive, they, who once showed so much honey, would now show their stings; but losers may have leave to talk, they have a proverb to their friend [?], it is a liberty due to their fortune. Yet, as to the management of yourself, I would have you suppress your gall as you have cleared your liver;[69] let not their

---

68 i.e. seize opportunities by the forelock – they are bald behind. (*OED*)
69 Anciently thought to be the seat of love.

anger move yours; and so by the conquest of two passions, your victory will be complete, and their thunder will never hurt your laurel.[70] I believe it gave them no little trouble to see you move with such solid steps, to see your understanding so much beyond your years that you carried your love in a string, and could neither be so moulded by their wills nor touched by the magnet of their high caresses, but that you would sometimes point into the vale and follow the direction of your true friend. Though the person and portion (if well secured) were without exception, yet for your sake I disliked the match, ab origine, because not only your hopeful abilities would have been checked and lost, but the whole pleasure and happiness of your life would have suffered shipwreck and been totally split upon that rock.

Had I seen any advantage, nay had I not forseen many ill aspects which might have arisen from the conjunction of our two planets, I should neither have been so straight in your maintenance nor so slow in the progress, you had had a bigger freight and the business a wider sail.

I shall close all with this wish: may you be successful within and without; may you have a thriving head and a growing fortune, which in the eyes of men are the two chief pillars of reputation, and like the poles in your globe support the esteem of the world. I may assure you this is a wish that proceeds not from ambition and avarice, but from the judicious thoughts, the unlimited love, and the deserved care of

Dear Willy,

Thy most affectionate Father,

W.L.

POST-SCRIPT TO LETTER 28

Willy left Oxford in 1687 to study at the Middle Temple[71] and an (undated) letter in the manuscript suggests that he may have subsequently been given patronage by 'the Right Honourable John Lord L'. Lawrence thanks the latter for the 'many favours with which you have been pleased so frequently to honour both myself and my son . . . '. 'My son,' continues Lawrence, in fulsome language, 'as if his genius were naturally shaped for your service, hath always had such an entire esteem for your Lordship, that he could not be satisfied but by drawing nearer to your person . . . '

70 Crown of poetic achievement.
71 Willy entered the Middle Temple on 10th February 1687/8. Lawrence, himself, entered on 7th November 1660 – having first entered Gray's Inn in 1654. (*Middle Temple Admissions Register* (3 Vols, L, 1949), Vol. 1. pp. 164, 222.)

LETTER 29

INTRODUCTION

King Charles II had died in 1685 and been succeeded by his brother, James II. Modern historians have been kinder to Charles II than were Lawrence and his Whig contemporaries. He has been given credit for being an astute politician and for his tolerance which did much to heal the wounds of the Civil War. He had fought to hand the Crown intact to his brother, though he knew him to be inept: 'I will take care to leave my Kingdoms to him in peace, wishing he may long keep them so. But this has all of my fears, little of my hopes, and less of my reason.' James II was able but inflexible.

With the reaction following the hysteria of the Exclusion crisis and the popularity of Charles II in his last 'golden days', James II ascended the throne with much goodwill. He survived the first test of his reign, the Monmouth rebellion – when the latter was defeated (at Sedgemoor) and subsequently beheaded – but the initial lack of opposition to Monmouth's campaign destroyed the King's confidence in the people's loyalty. His subsequent policy of giving official appointments to Roman Catholics, on whose loyalty he could rely, confirmed the electorate's worst fears. He removed Protestant officers and men from the Irish Standing Army, replacing them with Roman Catholics; brought some of these Irish, celtic-speaking regiments over to England and introduced Irish and English Roman Catholics into English regiments – a subject Lawrence treats with particular vehemence.

Lawrence was only a child when the Irish rebelled against the English and Scots settlers in 1641 but would have remembered more clearly Cromwell's severe response in 1649–50 when the old Irish landlords were dispossessed and the land given to men from Cromwell's Army. Some estates were returned at the Restoration but, as with the dispossessed landlords in England, the Crown had neither the means nor the ability to restore the pre-Cromwellian situation.

By now the Celts and the descendants of the original Norman, Roman Catholic, settlers (known as the 'Irish' and 'Old English' respectively) had largely merged their 400-year-old differences and united in opposition to the newer, sixteenth- and seventeenth-century, English-speaking, Protestant, settlers. These latter had ruled the Country, until ousted by James II, themselves temporarily forgetting the differences between the Church of Ireland and the dissenting Churches, in defence of their position.[72]

In April 1688, the King issued the second of two Declarations of Indulgence, which Lawrence had heard read in church that morning. Charles II had twice issued Declarations of Indulgence to 'tender consciences' to promote the toleration of both Roman Catholics and Dissenters. Twice, Parliament had reversed the Declarations and passed Test Acts (requiring proof of loyalty to the Church of England before being appointed to any official position) against the minority religions. James' Declaration, and his hopes of repealing the Test Acts,

---

72 A further group of 'Old English' settlers (to differentiate between them and the 'New English', and Scots, Protestant settlers), and who had gone over to Ireland in the Middle Ages, were to be found on both sides of the religious divide.

met with no more favour. Many in the Church, including the Archbishop of
Canterbury and six other bishops, objected (for which they were tried, though
acquitted, for 'seditious libel') – as does Lawrence. It is estimated that the
Declaration was read in only 200 of the many thousands of parish churches in
the Country – of which Badgeworth (Little Shurdington was in Badgeworth
parish) may, it seems, have been one.

At home, Anne is again recovering from what is obviously a serious illness.

LETTER 29

To Col: Henry Norwood   [Undated. May/June 1688][73]
[M.P. for Gloucester 1675]

Sir,
What between living alone and lying alone I had got so great a cold, that for
some days I have breathed nothing but enclosed air; but having at last shook
off the remora [impediment], I am now making haste to my best beloved,
whose distemper hath at present beat another parley, and given her some
respite from her double sorrow: for she hath laboured many months and
some years under the miseries of pain and physic but yet with such
admirable fortitude that I believe she can smile upon a rack, and lie gently
upon a bed of thorns, her natural spirit hath followed the precepts and
outdone the patience of a Stoic. If in the great volume of fate, the reason be
entered as well as the execution, I would fain know from those eternal
records, why a body and soul so exactly shaped or (which is much more)
why one so well fitted for the next life, should feel so many sorrows in this.
But fatis agimur, cedite fatis [we are driven by the fates, yield to them]; all
human bodies are bound up by invincible laws of fate; it is a necessity which
can neither be bowed by our prayers, nor broke by our power.

Our horses are summoned once more to the general muster [of the
Militia], though the King, fearing his subjects might unreasonably share his
royal title and prove the best Defenders of the Faith, hath very wisely
declared the Militia to be useless. But now I suppose that ancient service is
expired, and all our cold iron may be shortly turned into plough-shares.[74]

73 The letter is undated but would have been written at the end of May, if Lawrence was in
London, or the beginning of June, if he was in the country – the times when the Declaration,
first issued in April, was ordered to be read in the churches.
74 In his Speech from the Throne after the Monmouth rebellion, the King had said that it 'must
convince all men how little dependence could be placed on the Militia'. It was the excuse he
needed to raise further regiments for the Standing Army. (Since the Restoration, Parliament had
insisted on the Standing Army's being kept at a minimal level for fear of the power it would
give the King – and because of the hatred still felt for Cromwell's military rule.)

When Cato commanded a province in Spain to deliver up their arms, they laid it so to heart that they killed one another; they were ashamed to give up those weapons which they and their ancestors had long used for their honour and defence; and yet these were no free people, but were become slaves by conquest and the right of war.

When the sheep have delivered up their dogs, the Irish wolves may tear them at their pleasure and take possession both of their flesh and their fleeces. For the King now sets boldly up for St Patrick and St Peter; that old saint, and this new Father [Petre], will rule all;[75] the Irish must lead his Armies, and that daring priest must direct his councils and his conscience. But in the King and the priest I dare say there is nothing of the prophet, for else they might easily foresee they are but weaving of cobwebs, nets that have more art than strength, and when they come to be thrown out can never hold the civil and religious rights of three kingdoms.[76] The brains of the natural Irish art as soft as their bogs, and their manners as wild as their wolves:[77] they are . . . bred up to all sorts of villainy and fit for any tragic designs; their simplicity makes them bigots, and their fear makes them bloody. They have been always slaves and rebels to their old masters, but are now become the chief friends and darlings of the Crown and by a strange whim of fortune, they who once felt the whip, now shake it, and threaten revenge.

I went to church this morning to receive the sacrament and particularly the cup, not knowing how soon we may be reduced to a morsel of bread; for the Romish priest thinks that holy juice to be too rich for a layman, he takes the whole cup to himself, and puts the poor sinner off with a dry deified wafer. And here our timorous vicar (though against my advice) read the King's Declaration [of Indulgence]. The people you may think gave a very loyal attention, and were mightily pleased with his Majesty's promise to continue and increase his Army. Our bubbled clergy who were formerly so full of wind are now ready to break.[78] They have been so short-sighted, that their care, (in my judgment) should be removed from the pulpit to the poor or the highways, for of all people they are aptest to oversee.[79] And now, the

75 The Jesuit Father, Petre, Clerk of the Royal Closet, and one of the King's most influential advisers.
76 Prior to the Act of Union.
77 Wolves had become extinct in England during the reign of Elizabeth I, but existed in Scotland and Ireland until the 18th century.
78 i.e. with the return of a Roman Catholic monarch, and his attempts to 'Romanize' the Church of England, the Clergy must regret their opposition to the Exclusion Bill.
79 A play on the Surveyor of Highways and the Overseer of the Poor, who were village officials – the others were the Constable and the Churchwardens. (Before the introduction of toll-gates in the 18th century, the Surveyor of Highways was responsible for the upkeep of roads running through the Parish boundaries.)

more to expose their error and bridle their repentance, I hear the two dim lights of the Nation are to be speedily furnished with some troops of invincible arguments;[80] a head covered with steel will prove of much greater force than a head lined with logic.

But let things go how they will, I shall stick close to my centre, and follow no other magnet but that of our established laws and religion. The many variations of State may move my compassion, but can neither tempt the reason nor turn the resolution of

Sir,

your faithful servant

W.L.

King James II, as Duke of York
(detail), after Lely

80 A letter in the *Diary* refers to the 'two Eyes of the Nation' by which, Lawrence says, he means the two Houses of Parliament. The 'dim Lights' would therefore seem to translate as the 'short-sighted' Houses of Parliament. In 1688, James II had hoped to form a House of Commons and (by creating extra Peers) a House of Lords, sympathetic to his Declaration of Indulgence. The Lord President of the Council, the Earl of Sunderland, had suggested to Colonel Churchill: 'Oh, silly, your troop of Guards shall be called up to the House of Lords' – if they should prove intractable.

POST-SCRIPT TO LETTER 29

The exasperation shown in this letter was felt by both Whigs and Tories and when the second Declaration of Indulgence, in April, had been followed, in June, by the birth of a male heir, James Edward (to the King's second wife, Mary of Modena), this, by securing the Roman Catholic succession, renewed fears of permanent Roman Catholic domination. A secret letter, signed by a small group of influential Whigs and Tories, had been sent to Prince William of Orange inviting his armed assistance in persuading James to a more accommodating course and William, whose main aim in life was to frustrate Louis XIV's 'grand design' for Europe – agreed, largely out of fear that James would align himself with his fellow Roman Catholic monarch.

In the event, James panicked, fled to France on 23rd December 1688, and was deemed to have abdicated. The old inseparable fears: Roman Catholicism = absolutism = Louis XIV had prevailed.

William and Mary (James' elder, Protestant, daughter) were crowned as joint monarchs – although with reduced prerogative powers – an event that was hailed as a 'Glorious Revolution' both because it was bloodless (in England) and because, by and large, it had united both Whigs and Tories. (The more extreme Tories remained Jacobite just as the more extreme Whigs were Republican.)

LETTER 30

This is the first of three letters to Anne Fairfax, Anne Lawrence's greatest friend.

Anne, who is the daughter of the writer, Sir Thomas Browne, and her husband, Henry Fairfax, lived at Hurst Lodge – the third of the larger houses at Hurst – together with Hurst Place (the home of Sir Richard Harrison – the recipient of letter 19) and Haines Hill (the home of Lawrence's hated brother-in-law, John Bigge).

LETTER 30

For Madam Anne Fairfax[81]   January 28th 1691[2]

Madam,

As are the laws of the Crown, so are the methods of friendship, the King will not lose a subject without enquiring into the cause of his death;[82] I know you have the same desire in the case of your departed friend, and I am as eager to give you a short satisfaction.

My wife when she went to London began to swell with a dropsy, but that inundation of water was reduced, . . . and to her great content she died of a consumption. But though her body was much wasted, yet her face with very little diminution preserved the same air, and her eyes their usual vigour.

On the 11th January though she expected a speedy change, yet she sat at table with some invited friends, and was almost as brisk and pleasant as you have at any time seen her. Only her lips gave a presage of some sudden alteration, their courage could not keep pace with hers, but would sometimes tremble at their approaching dissolution. In the evening she retired into her chamber and spent some time with her son alone; telling him that her distemper with her life were now near a conclusion, and that she would set apart the next day to deliver her mind to us all and take her last farewell. But in the morning she felt the fatal stroke, and died as gently as an infant breathes. In this dissolution of nature and when her heat and colour had forsook her, she lay with such a lovely smile that I kept her face ten days uncovered. She never despised life nor feared death; she taught us how to live and how to die.

I carried the body down to Sherington, and there lodged all that remained of that dear person whom, when living, your unerring judgment had long declared to be the perfection of conjugal love, virtue, beauty, wit. Madam,

---

81 Anne's husband, Henry Fairfax, was the grandson of Viscount Fairfax of Emely, in Ireland (not the Lord Fairfax of Cameron of Cromwellian fame).
82 Sir Robert Filmer's 'Patriarcha' had been published in 1680 – a royalist argument for a monarchy based on the 'natural law of a father'.

you were the lady whom she esteemed beyond all others, and I always thought your souls to be so agreeable as if they had been cast in the same mould; she prized your person, the freedom of your humour, your very obliging and sociable temper beyond all that she had ever seen. And for that reason, Madam, and as the very figure of yourself, I recommend her memory to yours, and know she cannot lie in a nobler monument.

The ring I send is by her own direction with these letters, A.L. to A.F. – the circle represents eternity, and shows that she hath changed this transitory life for one that hath no end; where there are treasures brighter and richer than this best of metals, and in which I cannot but wish you an equal share with your lost friend. But that the time may be late, and left to your own election is the devout and shall be the daily petition of

Madam

your most faithful Servant

W.L.

LETTER 31

Madam,

Receiving intimation from my son that he was suddenly surprised with a violent fever, I made haste to London, where I at the same time met with your letter, and the hopes of his recovery. He had taken some doses of the Cortex [bark] before I came, a method of cure which I never much approved, because it often miscarries either by some accidents in the body, or for want of a judicious application. But if it prove successful, it will make me remember the different invention of the monk and the Jesuit: how the former by his powder ruins mankind, and the latter repairs it: if that violently breaks into one flame, this doth as gently extinguish or suppress another.[83] The doctor doth often and with much confidence affirm, that the danger is over, and his life secure.

Madam, my mother[84] informs me that you were pleased to wish for

Anne Lawrence, by Johann Kerseboom
painted *c.* 1691. The painting is
entitled *Anne Martin daughter of James
Martin*

---

83 The Franciscan friar, Roger Bacon (1214–92), is reputed to have discovered gunpowder. Cinchona, which came to be called 'Jesuit Bark' from the Jesuits who brought it to Europe, was first used in Peru. One product of the bark is quinine. Charles II's cousin, Prince Rupert, had refused 'Jesuit Bark' in his last illness, which perhaps confirms that its reputation was not high.
84 Lawrence's mother-in-law, Mrs Martin. His own mother had died in 1662.

something that belonged to your deceased friend. To present you with pearl or diamonds were but to throw a spark into a flame; you so abound in jewels, that their meaner lustre would be lost, and I should but vainly endeavour to make you brighter than you are. And therefore to come nearer to your request, I have presumed to send you a double remembrance and which I thought would be more acceptable than any present of a much greater value. It is a laced handkerchief and a ring: the one was often in her hand, the other always upon her finger. My dear wife was your faithful servant, and this ring was hers, for in her lifetime it was always at hand, and at her death stuck close to her finger, when her very breath, the best and the last friend of life had forsook her.

I hear that my brother B. [John Bigge] continues his old churlish nature, and that his son whom I sent home with a better expectation was at first refused, and then received, and then removed. Men's thoughts are full of variety and uncertain resolutions: but yet there is one head that, while it points at your service, hath no vane upon it, which is that of

Madam

Your most faithful Servant,

Wm. Lawrence.

LETTER 32

For Madam Anne Fairfax   March 16th 1691/2

Madam,
Your most obliging letter finds me entering into my second scene of sorrow,
and carrying my beloved son to his last repose. I know you will think that
my heart is as heavy as the lead he lies in, and that two such tragic strokes
are enough to tire any patience though never so well fortified with reason
and religion. In one month I lost your friend: and within two more my son:
the former did only divide the body and took away a dear life, but this latter
cuts through the very roots and extirpates a posterity: in her I lost a wife, but
in him a family, that bowed my heart, but this can do no less than break it.
As his mother died, so died he: they both left the world with a smile, as if
Death were either proud of his victory, or they pleased with their new
prospect.

Your happy temper seems so generously inclined to friendship and
compassion, that I have presumed to disturb your smoother thoughts with
these rough and mournful accents, but, Madam, I will for a while stop this
loud torrent of my grief, and silently contemplate the vanities of this world
and all the bubbles of human life. My son's picture was first drawn and then
my wife's; they are so excellently done that they seem to continue that life
which they resigned: the former I have sent down, the latter at your request I
leave behind me, that you may see all that remains of her, and therein
observe how our best delights end in shadows, and how our most solid
felicities at last steal away and leave nothing behind them but a cold
remembrance. Their lives and their pictures were finished near the same

'*Et genus et pectus*'

85 Lawrence carried out this intention. The portrait, by Johann Kerseboom, on p. ii (detail
above) shows him pointing to his broken heart surrounded by his coat of arms, itself broken.
The inscription reads: 'Et Genus et Pectus' (both heart and descent).

time, which makes my grief incline me to have mine too, for, as if there were the guilt of a petty treason in my family, we are first to be drawn, and then immediately executed.[85]

I am sorry to hear of my brother's [again John Bigge's] stubborn resolution, and that he should not only slight his own children but those that love 'um; how base and deformed is that temper, which lays aside honour, civility, friendship, and natural affection. When I sent his son home, I bid my man wait upon you, but the brutish reception which he had at the Hill, [Haines Hill] made him hasten away to his old vale and neglect his commission.

But Madam, I must draw to a conclusion, for the consideration of your tender expressions and my repeated losses draw a cloud into my eyes, and a faint pulse at my heart begins to shake the hand of

Madam

Your very sad but very faithful Servant

W.L.

LETTER 33

Lawrence becomes a recluse at Shurdington but, in his grief, lashes out at the only person on whom he can lay the blame for Willy's death – Dr Edward Browne.

Edward Browne is the eldest son of Sir Thomas Browne and, therefore, the brother of Anne Fairfax. It is curious that Lawrence writes of 'the doctor' and not 'your brother' when writing to Anne – a connection of which he was aware. Perhaps he is trying to distance social and professional relationships.

Edward Browne (1644–1708) was considered an upright and conscientious man in which, according to the *Dictionary of National Biography*, he resembled his father, although he did not have Sir Thomas' 'deeper strain of thought'. He was a fellow of the Royal Society and physician to the King.

LETTER 33

For Dr Edw: Browne   March 22nd 1691[2]

Sir,

When I met the body of my dear friend, and saw those crowds of people who gazed as at a prodigy upon those mournful remains, I made a strict enquiry into all the circumstances of his death; but the sad and odd account that was given me of it, made me then shed many tears, and now send many miles to ask you this question: why you would so betray and flatter a young gentleman out of his life? A youth who was much known for his many virtues, and is as much lamented. It was a saying of Vespasian, Oportet Imperatorem stantem mori [an emperor should die standing up];[86] and as if you designed my friend for a hero, his garments by your direction were put on a little before his death, and he expired in his clothes.

Either you knew the whole progress of his danger, or you knew it not: if you did not know it, it is a blot upon your judgment: if you did, it is a stain upon your humanity. For by a confidence which continued from his first to his last hours, you made him not only neglect other helps and his temporal affairs, but in some measure slacken those pious inclinations which he always had to secure his future hopes. If this be Religio Medici,[87] I know the shape of his foot [cloven?] (unless it be a vulgar error) who may lay an unquestioned claim to the whole faculty.

The surgeon (it seems) understood the mistake and presaged his danger: the apothecary indeed thought he might have lasted much longer being so

---

86 Quoted in Suetonius, *Life of Vespasian*, 24.
87 The writer, Sir Thomas Browne, Edward Browne's father (who was also a physician) wrote *Religio Medici* (A Doctor's Faith). It was published in 1643.

thoroughly powdered. It is further said in this case (as it hath happened in many more) that you might perhaps perceive the danger, but yet would hide it, lest by a consultation with other learned heads they might observe the error, and see and censure this new method of killing. The physicians, beyond the prerogative of princes have an arbitrary power of life and death; in that profession alone killing is no murder; they can destroy men and families at pleasure and no law can reach 'um; which makes me start a little from the rules of religion, and think how happy Alexander was, who had the power to revenge the untimely fate of his beloved Hephaestion.[88]

But my dear friend, forsaking his old staff to lean upon a new reed, is now gone beyond recovery: my complaints and my sighs are vain, the dreadful loss is not to be repaired either by my sorrows or your repentance: and therefore my chief design of writing this is for the benefit of those whom you shall find to resemble him in youth, hopes, and merit: I mean, that in your future practice you may not play with such a life, but use more judgment, more care and more conscience.

And so God direct your heart and ease mine; for if you will listen to the discourse of the town, never any private gentleman died better beloved or more lamented.

Ab Ignoto.

Sir Thomas Browne, author of
Religio Medici and father of Anne
Fairfax and Dr Edward Browne

Dr Edward Browne

88 Hephaestion, the Macedonian General and greatest friend and brother-in-law of Alexander the Great. Alexander is said to have ordered that the doctors attending Hephaestion in his last illness should be hung.

PART II

'Let friendship succeed nature . . .'

LETTER 34

INTRODUCTION

Two new characters enter the scene: Judge William Powlett and Sir Michael Hicks, who become Lawrence's most frequent correspondents in the succeeding years. They visit him, advise him – most frequently to remarry – and keep him informed.

Six months after Willy's death, Sir Michael Hicks, who is a near neighbour in Gloucestershire, writes to Lawrence, from London, of the news circulating in the coffee houses of the City. The talk at the time was of William III's campaigns. Between 1689 and 1692, King James II, with French assistance, sought to regain his throne by landing and fighting in Ireland. The war, which had begun with the siege of Londonderry (when the Protestants were relieved, just in time, by the ships from England) and ended with the siege of Limerick (when the Roman Catholics were not relieved in time by the ships from France) had been mainly decided by the battle of the Boyne, in 1690, when James II had been defeated, fled the field, and retired to France. King William III was now free to pursue his main aim of opposing Louis XIV on the Continent.

Meanwhile, Lawrence's company is sought by at least one 'beauty' hopeful of taking Anne's place.

LETTER 34

For Sir Michael Hicks[1]   October 7th 1692

Sir,
You inform me that you and your whole retinue are returned safe to London. The thought of so many kind visits and so many kind receptions makes me equally sensible of that felicity which I once had, and which I now want. But yet I am not singly unhappy, for the face of nature is changed, and every thing begins to put on a solitary aspect, though March hath a rough voice,

---

1 Sir Michael Hicks (1645–1710) was the second son of Sir William Hicks, 1st Bt., of Ruckholts, in Essex, and Beverstone Castle, in Gloucestershire. Sir William had a dubious record in the Civil War but seems to have convinced himself that he had suffered in the Royalist cause. Charles II knighted both of the sons – Sir Michael, who was only 18 or 19 at the time, and his elder brother, William, to satisfy any expectation of reward.

Sir Michael's father settled some property on him in 1674, which included Witcombe Park (3 miles from Shurdington) and a house in London. Sir Michael was educated at Oxford, was married and, like Lawrence, lived a life of leisure, spending his summers at Witcombe and the winter in London.

(*A Cotswold Family: Hicks and Hicks-Beach* by Mrs William Hicks-Beach, 1909, William Heinemann)

89

yet the following months breathe mild and low; but October and all that succeed him speak fierce and loud; and as if Boreas[2] were some mighty Prince, the trees not only tremble when he roars, but the leaves fall from their heads, and nothing must stand covered before him; which makes me observe how while the rational part of the world begins to defend themselves by clothes and fire, the vegetative throw off their apparel, and with naked limbs expect all the hardships of winter.

I thank you for the news you sent me, and hope your supposition will guide the success: the topping genius of the King, like that of Augustus, makes the rest shrink and tremble; James trusts more in his feet than his arms, he always feared and fled. Lewis [Louis] confides in the covert of his camp and lies safely entrenched; he mines only with his gold, and fights by surprise.[3] Like a wary dog, he barks at a distance, and sometimes bites in the rear; and so will continue to do and no otherwise, till some bold and fortunate attempt can break into his Country, and by the ruin or revolt of his cities, can either muzzle or chain up that great enemy of mankind.[4]

I can make no exchange of news, the surprise of a partridge or the pursuit of a hare are the utmost attacks that are made in these parts. I went last week a coursing but not far from home, in the company of a great beauty; she had not my Lady's [Hick's?] fortune, the hare died in her view, but not at her feet; he with his life lost his liberty; but I had not one thought soft enough to betray mine. Age hath not yet turned me to touchwood; I find my temper is not yet so dry as to be touched with any sparks of love; they may flutter about me, but not fasten. This fair lady says she will visit me again in the Spring, perhaps she thinks my blood will then grow warmer, and my optics will more narrowly gaze upon her charms. But my heart lies as secure as a mark at Rovers;[5] many may shoot, but none can hit; Cupid may empty his whole quiver, and not find one arrow that can pierce it.

That our amity may continue firm, and our letters frequent, is the only desire that at present warms the breast of

Sir,

Your faithful Servant.

W.L.

2 The God of the North Wind.

3 Laying siege to, and mining, the enemy's fortifications was the most common form of warfare at the time. By October, there was a halt in the fighting until the following Spring – when Lawrence suggests that Louis is using financial influence to further his ambitions.

4 The King had hoped to invade France but this idea was abandoned for the time being after his attack (at Steenkirk), two months earlier, had been severely repulsed.

5 Used, as here, metaphorically – 'virtually impossible to hit'. Derived from a randomly placed target designed to train the eye to judge distance.

LETTER 35

Writing to Judge William Powlett, Lawrence explains how he is spending his time. He is engaged in designing and creating a garden at Shurdington in memory of five generations of his family and, in particular, of Anne and Willy. The idea was, perhaps, suggested to him by Sir Michael Hicks who was completing his house at Witcombe and laying out the park and gardens at the time. Lawrence encloses the first of two descriptions of his memorial garden, both of which are in the Appendix.

The letter is written on Christmas Day – his first without Anne and Willy. It is no longer a red-letter day.

LETTER 35

For William Powlett Esq;[6]   December 25th 1692

Sir,

I received yours on Christmas Eve; it came to usher in the Nativity and was as welcome as the jolly time that succeeds it. I thank you for your late kind visit; we may both very justly complain, you for your mean reception, and I for your short stay; but I hope to see them both mended another day, when your great business, and my better fortune shall incline you to cut me out a larger proportion of time.

I have at present no oves nor boves [sheep and cattle], but I have a longer rhyme in as few syllables; the plough, the mow, the cow, and the sow, are some part of my diversion, the rest is made up in the execution of many solitary thoughts. You think the oves and boves take up all my time, and therefore invite me to a better society. As to this latter the case is altered: I am at most ease when alone, and my best enjoyment is to have none; for my late losses have made so sharp an impression that they have given me a total aversion to society and all the reasons that may induce it. As to the former, melancholy (in which by nature and misfortune I have a double share) is a kind of sleepy humour, and that you may see how I drowse away my time I have sent you the enclosed [the description of the garden]. Upon the death of my wife and son, both of them destroyed by the physician, I entered into this matter, and having little to do, drew it into this form. You are a real

---

6   William Powlett (or Pawlet, –1703), a bachelor, was the son and heir of George Powlett of Borceston, in Warwickshire. He was called to the Bar from the Middle Temple in 1660 – two years earlier than Lawrence – so their friendship may date from this time. William Powlett was made a Judge in 1689. He was also deputy Warden of the Forest of Dean and deputy Constable of St Briavel's forest (the only part of the original Forest still in existence today) – which appointments would have given him the opportunity to visit Lawrence from time to time.

judge in some things and an able judge in all, but I desire you would read the enclosed not with the severity of a judge, but with the indulgence of a friend. I send it only to clear your doubt of what I am doing; and I the rather send it, because it will come between the two [Law] terms, and at a festival, when I presume you lay aside all public business.

I hope you will follow the common example, and wear away the twelve days with much mirth and pleasure: it is a time of liberty, wherein a religious custom makes the world spread their brows, and look with cheerful aspect. But no red letter falls to my share: I once thought my future life would have been very smooth, and that I should have possessed many albos dies, days as white as my paper; but I find the colour to be changed, they are now nigro carbone notati, and as black as that ink wherein I subscribe the name of Sir,

your faithful Servant

W.L.

LETTER 36

INTRODUCTION

William Powlett has apparently written trying to persuade Lawrence into remarriage. There is even an oblique suggestion that he (or, as it is put, a mutual friend) should invest a future wife's dowry in a good investment he has in mind. This was the fund known as the 'Million Adventure' – one of several schemes whereby Parliament sought to raise funds (some by lottery) for the war against France. Two years later, a similar scheme financed the founding of the Bank of England.

LETTER 36

For Wm. Powlett, Sergeant at Law,[7]   Jany 15. 1692[3]
and one of the Judges of Wales

Sir,

In the size of your letter I see, (not without some concern) the great trouble I gave you. My case is so very well and thoroughly argued, that your advice shall be improved into a command and I will obey it as far as I can; the rest I leave to time, which in these kind of losses always produceth those effects which all the arguments from general topics of reason and religion can never reach. I know if I would follow the common methods of the living, it is easy to renew my condition, though hard to repair it: for if I get another wife, I may perhaps not get another son; or if both, yet it is only superis notum, qui pueri, qualisque futura sit uxor [the Gods know what sons and what sort of wife we will have]:[8] it is a secret above, which may be only opened by experience: and hath a doubtful event: they may be neither neatly formed nor strongly built; either more meanly qualified, or shorter lived. Nay, these fine materials so well collected by nature and the thread so finely spun by education, may at last be coarsely handled and cut by the hand of the physician. In fine when I look back upon all my paternal cares and fears, and how the vast hopes of many years were broken in one single minute, pudet me genuisse mortalem [I am shamed that I have born a mortal];[9] and I will make no further trial.

You tell me of a fund for raising a million and that you advise our friend F.H. to marry quickly, and throw in the whole portion; but he is now grown

---

7 An ancient order from which all Judges were drawn – roughly equivalent to today's Q.C.
8 Juvenal, *Satires* 10, 352–3.
9 Lawrence's meaning is not altogether clear here. Apparently adapted from Ovid *Metamorphoses* 10.217 or *Tusculan Disputations* 3.30 (the latter had 'sciebam me genuisse mortalem' – 'I knew that I had fathered a mortal'. This is nearer to his thought in letter 38 when he says acceptance of death is a condition for entry to life.).

an old bird and having made it the diversion of 30 years to rage fiercely against matrimony, he will hardly be persuaded to sell his liberty for 7 per cent, or enter into that politic noose, where he must spend some weeks in wooing and all the rest of his life in cooing, like two conjugal doves in a cage. When the flesh grows so fast, the spirits decrease; he is a size too big and perhaps too weak for such a bold attempt. Let him think of what he did in his former days and that will be lechery enough for his short breath, weight and years.

Increase and multiply was the first blessing: he and you have always shunned the offer, and I have sought and possessed it in vain; I am left as naked as you, and like the condition of a celibate I have nothing to love, and nothing to fear. Let friendship succeed nature, this is all the enjoyment that I wish for, and all that is now left to

Sir,

Your faithful Servant

W.L.

'like two conjugal doves in a cage'

LETTER 37

To Sir Michael Hicks   January 16th 1692/3

Sir,

I wish myself with you but to no purpose, for wishes are things that give wings to the thought and nothing else. I acknowledge that your wine is very good; that the juice of the grape exceeds the coarser spirit of barley, and that the City in a splendid manner can feast the King and their own eyes. Luxury is there in its richest habit and hath a tempting variety. But yet (to make the gist of my retirement) I must tell you, that we don't run to the coffee house to discover in that cloud of smoke, who 'tis that was killed today, or what town must be attacked tomorrow; while you impatiently ramble abroad for news, we sit quietly at home to expect it. Your contrary hopes are backed with wagers and you live in anxiety till the doubt be decided. If the foreign post be delayed you are uneasy and hardly sleep that night. The City is as full of vices as Amsterdam of religions,[10] their morals are more stained and

Sir Michael Hicks

10 This may refer to Kid's coffee-house, known as 'Amsterdam', which attracted such customers as Titus Oates, the inventor of the 'Popish Plot'.

spotted than a leopard while the country puts on the garb of innocence, and is at this hour as white as the snow can make it. A surplice or a lawn sleeve when new washed and in the height of devotion is not more free from spots.

But to tell you some news, this snow sets up a new way of hunting; the scent is of no use; the poachers are all abroad and the dogs at home: one ear up and another down [his own dog?] is now of little advantage. The swiftness of the hare's foot once carried her off with success but now the print of those very feet discover and betray her.

Another mischief is, this weather will bring no more fair ladies to my house; and that little fire that is left in my veins will be so checked by the outward cold, that I shall look abroad for none; but e'en pass away the long chill nights as chaste and retired as a hermit.

. . . You say there are critical minutes in love; but I find there are critical minutes in letters as well as love; for last night when I writ this, the earth was deep covered with snow; but before morning it was (like the declining fiat of a battle) almost totally routed by the warm assault of a south wind; and by this noon it is all run away. Only here and there some scattered parties appear on the sides of the hills or else sheltered under the covert of a hedge: but there is now a flying squadron of rain sent out in the pursuit, which (in the words of the Gazette) will soon give a good account of those broken troops.

LETTER 38

INTRODUCTION

It is the anniversary of Willy's death and Dr Browne receives a second letter.

LETTER 38

For Dr Edw: Browne   March 8th 1692/3

Sir,

This unhappy day finished a young life and a long descent. I do not mourn so much at his death, for, hac conditione intravit [he entered (life) on this condition]; as that he should be cast away when the pilot so confidently affirmed that the coast was free from rocks and thoroughly sounded. But that which strikes deepest and gives me a waking grief, is, that having much to say and much to do, he was so flattered with this assurance that he was persuaded to defer not only his meaner concerns but his much desired and best preparations. And if the omission of a duty be like the commission of a sin, I may then compare it to that Italian, who first debauched his enemy, and then destroyed him.[11]

My charity is too great to wish you or any man the weight of my sorrows. Nor do I write this only to rub up your memory and keep your conscience free from slumbers, but to ease my afflicted thoughts of that heavy burden under which they daily sigh and labour; for a working heart like a fermenting vessel, must sometimes have vent, or else it may swell till it break itself and the very hoops that enclose it.

Ab Ignoto.

11 An 'Italian' derives from the Renaissance flowing script, replacing the old Gothic script, and came to be used metaphorically as: 'the hand of such a man can be discerned in that deed'. It is possible that Lawrence is referring to the Buckingham-Shrewsbury scandal in letter 12 ('the Duke first stained his blood, and then spilt it'). As Physician to the King, Dr Browne would have been familiar with the Court gossip.

LETTER 39

For Sir Michael Hicks 1692

Sir,

. . . I kept the Thanksgiving[12] after a new mode: roast beef to all comers and at night a very light supper; for every light in the front of my house had three candles, in all above 300; so that if the people had not a great, yet they had at least a splendid entertainment: and with so much good will, that with the addition of one word, I could make the motto of one of our great luminaries to be mine, Deus et Rex illuminatio mea [God and the King are my light].[13] These illuminations being a novelty in these parts, my house at a distance seemed as if it were in a flame, which some came to see and some to extinguish.

But Ned[14] was not there, the sins of his youth began to steal upon him; the gout had caught him by the foot. To talk smutty to him now and to tread on his toe is equally pleasing. With the gout entered another hot fit, a fit of devotion; when his toe aches his knee bends and he asks forgiveness for many things which he don't remember. One swingeing fit of the gout will make a greater penitent in an hour than the lungs of the pulpit in a whole year.

May our limbs be active to the last minute, and if we must be lame let us come to our crutches by the course of nature. And that it may be the effect of our age, and not of our vices is both for your sake and my own the common petition of

Sir,

your faithful Servant

W.L.

'when his toe aches, his knee bends'

12 For the accession of William & Mary.
13 The motto of Oxford University is 'Dominus' (not 'Deus') 'illuminatio mea'.
14 The use of his Christian name suggests a member of the household – perhaps the steward.

LETTERS 40 & 41

INTRODUCTION

In a letter to William Powlett, Lawrence sums up his perception of a barrister's life – the life he himself spurned 30 years earlier – and, in a second letter, looks forward to welcoming the Judge to his own preferred way of life at Shurdington.

The Judge seems to be planning to retire to Shurdington and lodge with Lawrence – much as the Lawrences once lived with first, John Bigge, and then Sir Richard Harrison, at Hurst.

LETTER 40

To William Powlett   Feb. 12th 1693

. . . The client racks you [the barrister] with many impertinent questions, and opens his purse as you encourage his cause; the attorney must be humoured, and treated and courted, or else the grist may be carried to another mill: and if you are not the son, or nephew of the Judge your argument is of little force, and you must either marry his favour, or buy it, or lose it. If you are too forward at the Bar, the Judge grows froward [perverse] at the Bench; if you plead too coldly, the client fears and dislikes you; if too warmly, the Judge frowns and checks you. If honour be your aim, and you endure all this that you may be at last covered with skins and scarlet, the way is so rough and long before you can come to this grave figure, that methinks, it looks like an object at the wrong end of the perspective, the distance makes it seem very small and not to be regarded. I remember these were some of my many reasons why I slighted that study. . . .

'the Judge grows froward'

LETTER 41

March 15th 1692/3

... But yet I find that in this long pursuit after wealth and honour, you have got one treasure and lost a greater. You complain of the decay of your health, and that the Temple air, like your business, is too thick. For this reason, you long to be in this wide prospect, and to share in the refined air which I breathe. Sir, I think you have pitched upon an air that hath produced many long lives, and may contribute much to the security of yours; it hath neither the sharpness of the hill nor the moistness of the vale; we see the fogs, but feel 'um not; they are either above us or below us. And therefore I now assure you that you shall be very welcome whenever the Bar and the Bench can spare you; your society and our ancient friendship are a full satisfaction in themselves and we need treat of no other terms.

But if you will give me notice of the hour of your coming, that I may have some oil in my lamp and not be taken unprovided, it will be another obligation to

     Sir,

         your faithful Servant

         W.L.

LETTER 42

In the Nine-Years War of 1688–97, William III had not only his new British Kingdoms to support him, but Austria, Spain, many of the German Principalities and Savoy. Their combined aim was to push back the French frontiers and to uphold the Austrian claim to the Spanish Netherlands. (The ageing Charles II of Spain was childless and his inheritance was claimed by both Austria and France.) Parliament was content to support the King through fear of a French invasion to reinstate James II and to protect England's trade against the rising power of the French Navy. Lawrence, nevertheless, complains of the extra expense that the war entails.

At last Lawrence and the Whigs have a monarch to their liking and whose fortunes on the Continent they follow with high expectation of success. Their total confidence in the 'topping genius' of the King was misplaced. Although the most effective of Louis XIV's opponents, William's success in Ireland against James II was not matched by equal success against the superior strategy of France's Duke of Luxembourg.

William III was not universally popular. Described as 'small, dark and asthmatic', James II, on first meeting him as a potential son-in-law, decided he was 'badly brought up'. Some resented his using the man-power and wealth of his new Kingdoms to protect the Netherlands and resented his neglect of the Queen, who was much loved.

LETTER 42

For Sir Michael Hicks   March 29th 1693

Sir,

The long consultations of the winter are now ripening into action,[15] for you tell me that the King declared he would be at Portsmouth on Friday last, and therefore I conclude him gone; for he can neither break a promise made to others nor to himself. His very words are actions, when he deliberates, he resolves; when he resolves, he executes. But on Saturday the wind began to rise and continued for some days very fierce and high; a presage (if he be gone) that he will shake his enemy, as the wind shakes him; and that this storm was sent for no other reason than that he might carry it over with him, and throw it upon the opposite shore.

March and the King go out like a lion: the arms of the House of Orange, the Belgick and the British arms are all lions: these he carries in his banners, but he bears a fiercer in his breast. Richard the First had not a greater heart.

---

15 It was the King's practice to confer with his Ministers in London during the winter before embarking for the continent in the Spring to renew his campaigning. 1693 was, in fact, one of the worst years of the war for William and his allies, both on land and sea.

He succeeds a lazy race of Princes, a race unlike his own and so given up to ease and venery, that he seems not so much destined to possess the throne as to strengthen and reform it. He hath our old enemy the French to deal with, an enemy that hath been often and notably foiled in former ages; and why not now, since in his single person are revived the courage, activity, and martial genius of all our ancient Kings? And to sharpen these virtues he fights for the common liberty of Europe; he aims not at the increase of dominion, but only to humble the ambition of that vain monarch, who is the hostis humani generis [the enemy of the human race]; who like the hawk is always in arms, and without distinction preys upon every thing that is weaker than he.

And now while the country looks green, we may expect the camp will be stained with another colour; while the trees put forth their buds, the cannon will fling forth their bullets, and the sword will cut men off faster than we can get 'um. The bed of marriage will hardly supply the bed of honour. However it is much safer to sit in the pit than to act upon the stage; better to hear and see at a distance, than to be a party in those tragic scenes; methinks London having the first tumultuous news of fights and sieges, lies within the noise of the drum and the cannon; it seems a little too near the seat of war; and therefore I hope you will hasten hither, where we have it more gently delivered and at second hand, like the fainting voice of an echo. Bleeding is very useful in the Spring[16] but while the soldier opens the vein, 'tis we that pay the surgeon; he holds the sword, but 'tis our money must whet it.

King William of Orange, after J. van Wyck

16 To rid the body of accumulated 'humours' that caused disease.

Ned is still in a declining condition and hath in one month run through a whole gauntlet of diseases, and I think will hardly repulse such a general assault. He is weak in body and heart. Fortem posce animum, et mortis terrore carentem [ask for a heart which is brave and without fear of death]:[17] one great blessing of life, is, always to expect death, and never to fear it. Whether it come by age or sickness or grief, I look upon it as the divine decree, and not so much a dissolution as an exchange of life. Bene vivere et fortiter mori [to live well and to die bravely], is the best wish I can give myself and the best that can be bestowed upon my friend by

Sir,

your faithful Servant

W.L.

17 Juvenal, *Satires* 10, 357.

LETTER 43

INTRODUCTION

At the beginning of the campaigning year, the King is due to return to London but without the hoped-for success against France – and another 'fair lady' (or perhaps the same one, at whose feet neither the hare nor Lawrence fell) accepts defeat.

LETTER 43

For Wm. Powlett Esq;   October 27th 1693

Sir,

I am sorry the King is not yet embarked. Fortune hath lately shifted her sails, and which is more he upon whom the winds used to wait[18] now waits for a wind; 'tis pity his heroic heart can't fix a chain upon that wandering jilt, and make her a constant slave to his great designs. Merit and success are seldom coupled together long; he hath this Summer suffered both in his allies and his own arms: valour was every where oppressed by number, and he that deserved a triumph, returns with the only honour of being admired for his personal courage and conduct. It was rightly observed that single thieves are punished, while the greater robberies when committed by an armed power are applauded, Ille Crucem pretium Sceleris tulit hic Diadema [one gets the Cross for his crime, another the Crown]:[19] that which is villainy in a private man, is glory in a Prince. The French King thinks that for men to obey other Princes is to taste of the forbidden fruit, and therefore, with his flaming sword, he drives whole nations from the paradise of peace and plenty; it equally kills and burns; no reason can stop his rage, nor can any force as yet repulse his ambition. Attila who was styled the flagellum Dei [the scourge of God][20] was not a greater tyrant, he only whipped the nations and away, but this insatiable monarch designs a perpetual bondage and, if not stopped by our British hero, he will soon lash all the bordering provinces into a slavish subjection.

But to return home, my fair Lady K, is now going to London and our friend L.H. shall see her. Perhaps those charming features which have failed here may be successful there, he hath been long a bitter enemy to wedlock, and 'tis but a just revenge to see a fair face at last either bow his heart with love or break it with despair.

---

18 A reference to the 'protestant wind' that took King William's fleet across the channel in 1688 while holding King James' ships captive in the Thames estuary.
19 Juvenal, *Satires* 13, 105.
20 Attila, King of the Huns, laid siege to half of Europe during his rule between 435 and 453 A.D.

This morning our young ladies [of the household?] tell me that about midnight they heard a great hacking and hewing as if the masons had been returned to their labour: I was glad at the news hoping some kind spirits were come to ease me both in time and expense. But when I went to see how far the building was improved, I found it all as I left it; perhaps it might be a frolick of King Oberon, who with his train might be tripping round a stone, imitating the Cyclop's dance and keeping time with their little hammers. The pharisees [fairies], (as they call 'um here) had only a mind to be merry, and intended rather to play than work.

But while I build I decay, and while I am raising other's monuments, I draw nearer to my own: it is all but a Sic nos non nobis, [thus we (work) not for ourselves] and by that time I have done my business my business may be done: for I am sensible that I begin to wither, and that though I am heaping up many stones, I must shortly be contented with one.

I thank you for your distich upon my sun-dials, for fancies are as clear as that planet, and therefore fit for his daily observation, but I have already fixed there some of my own mottos, though I must confess our thoughts are very different, for yours resemble the light and mine the shade. To this I shall only add, that had I an opportunity to serve you, you alone should measure my remaining hours, the gnomons[21] should not be more steady and true to the sun than would be

your very faithful Servant,

Wm. Lawrence.

---

21 The rod or pin that casts a shadow on the sun-dial.

LETTER 44

INTRODUCTION

It is March 8th – a date that Dr Edward Browne can hardly have failed to anticipate.

LETTER 44

For Dr Edward Browne   March 8th 1693/4

He's gone and I shall never never see him more. This fatal day closed his eyes, and in one little short minute fell all my great hopes, his youth, his life, and his line. The sad habit is laid aside but the sad heart remains; I grow lighter without but darker within and time which takes off the edge and weight of other's sorrows doth but whet and increase mine, they are wide and sharp, very heavy and cut deep.

Our minds were as weak as his body, we thought all was safe under your great assurances; we relied too much in you, and you too much in yourself; and thus he unhappily fell by mistake. Which makes me send you this short remembrance that so by your being more nice and wary in such particular cases, the like violent fate may be prevented in other families, which is become an immedicabile vulnus[22] [incurable wound] and never to be cured in mine.

Anonymous

---

22 Ovid, *Metamorphoses* 10, 189

LETTER 45

INTRODUCTION

Sir Michael Hicks has lamented that the King and Queen have no heir. Maybe he introduced the subject in his efforts to persuade Lawrence into a second marriage – and himself produce an heir. The suggestion meets with a light, but firm, rebuff. The subject, it is clear, is closed.

LETTER 45

For Sir Michael Hicks   May 15th 1694

Sir,

You inform me that our King is got safe into Flanders, and that impatient of delay, he left his fleet many leagues from the shore and ventured in a single pinnace. The wind turned not to stop his voyage, but to increase his fame, for by this double daring he hath outdone Caesar in courage and fortune.

You admire his resolution, and wish he may not die without issue, and so do I: for 'tis great pity that posterity should see his picture only on his coin, and that such a race of heroes should expire. But I doubt when he should be vigorous in one attack, his mind runs after another, and that when his body is in the bed, his martial thoughts are in the field, which makes me sometimes fancy, that if the drums were beating and the trumpets sounding at his door in the time of coition, he would think himself engaged in an amorous war; and his genius being thus humoured he might perhaps make a home charge, and do the business with intention and success.

But as to the other part of your letter, wherein you tell me that your lady will try upon me the force of her more solid reason.[23] I know her thoughts are very fine, and her arguments weighty and persuasive, yet from the sense of my double loss, I think my resolution is fixed and I shall always continue in the same cool sullen humour. Cum aperto viverat horto [when (everyone) lived with an unwalled garden];[24] time was when there was no enclosure, when everyone had a right to all the fruits of the creation, and with a free appetite might walk through this seraglio of nature, and pick and taste where he pleased. But afterwards there came in a sort of amour, inde faces ardent, veniunt a dote sagittae [the dowry lit his fires, the dowry shot those

23 Lady (Susannah) Hicks was the daughter of Sir Richard Howe, a City Alderman, and the widow of Mr Samuel Everard, a barrister. 'Whatsoever Sir Michael's hand found to do (such as it was) he generally did with all his might, and there is no reason to suppose he sowed his wild oats with anything but supreme zest. And then, with all the good will in the world, he came to be thirty years old, and he took to wife a plump, dark-eyed, foolish woman . . . ' (A Cotswold Family, Mrs W. Hicks-Beach). Apart from the foolish wife, it all sounds much like William Lawrence's own youth.
24 Juvenal, Satires 6, 18.

arrows].[25] Avarice first, and then love began to set up for property; and mankind, rather than not have some thing which he might particularly call his own, weakly resigns his liberty, invents a long chain for himself, and makes his whole life a slave to his limited passion. If he had warily pitched upon the virtue by avoiding the extremes, he should neither have been loose to all, nor irrevocably confined to one.

If Matrimony like your Horn-tavern were a thoroughfare,[26] and one might enter, caress himself a while, and then go through at pleasure, there might be some encouragement for a second attempt. A man goes in souse [headlong] and with full vigour at the broad end, but is stopped at the narrow: and, in the emblem of suretyship, we see how simply a naked head peeps through the narrow end of a horn; it is pinched and straightened, looks about for relief, and struggles for liberty but all in vain.[27] In all my journeys I could never meet with any one who was travelling to Dunsmore.[28] And therefore I intend to husband my little remains of life and not like Sir Thomas[29] sacrifice all to the follies of a few nights, and at last give gold chains and medals to pacify expectation, and compound for my own weakness: plus aloes quam mellis habet [(a certain type of wife) has more bitterness than sweetness].[30]

But these reasons are only used for our mutual diversion, the prevailing argument is the tempus praeterlapsum [the intervening time]; when the evening is come, night will soon follow: my hair gives the first sign of decay and shows that I am setting; for some change their colour, and some desert. When the sap fails, the leaves fade and fall, and though the Spring may come on again, yet our lost youth and vigour returns no more.

And therefore that you may be happy in what you possess, and I contented in what I decline, is the settled and serious wish of

Sir,

your faithful Servant

W.L.

25 i.e. instead of Cupid. Juvenal, *Satires* 6, 139.
26 Unidentified but obviously a coaching inn with a central archway to admit the traveller.
27 'An emblem of suretyship' suggests a firemark – though none of this description is known – unless, of course, Lawrence means the face on the, best-known, Sun Assurance Company's emblem, 'pinched' by the sun's rays. The first fire-insurance companies dated from 1667 (after the Great Fire of London) and first issued firemarks – to identify properties covered by their companies – from *c.* 1680.

28 An expression denoting marital harmony. The tradition derived from the twelfth century. Any person travelling to Dunmow, in Essex, could claim a gammon of bacon (a Dunmow flitch) if, kneeling at the church door, he could swear he had never quarrelled with his wife, nor wished himself unmarried, for a year and a day. In five centuries, only eight people were so rewarded.
29 The only Sir Thomas who appears in the manuscript is Sir Thomas Lawrence, a cousin. As he is known to have wasted his inheritance (letter 50) this comment may well refer to him.
30 Juvenal, *Satires* 6, 181.

LETTER 46

INTRODUCTION

Queen Mary has died of smallpox – news which reaches Lawrence at an unfortunate time. His solution to the dilemma offers invention and malicious humour in equal measure.

LETTER 46

For Wm. Powlett Esq*re*   January 3rd 1694[5]

Sir,

Your hand and the print brought me a particular relation of the death of the Queen: very cold news, and in a very cold time; for meeting with a hard frost, much snow, and a keen air, the officina sanguinis[31] seemed to shut up shop, give over working, and feel a stupefaction beyond the relief of sherry: so that the many dozens you sent me, did perhaps rather please the palate, than warm the blood.

But for our mutual diversion and to fill this paper, I will give you a true though trivial account of my entertainment upon New Year's day. I had invited a great many of the shrubs of the state,[32] my tenants and some of my meaner [lesser] neighbours; but when they were all ready to enter into mirth and music, I received your letter and in it confirmation of the Queen's death. I thought the news was too sad for a merry meeting, and yet I knew those narrow souls would not be contented without it.

And so I took this course: I had a large flagon filled with decayed small beer, and then threw into it a good lump of ice; so that it was as dead and cold as the Queen; and having also poured into it a sufficient quantity of the spirit of wormwood, I then acquainted them with the sad news; and told them they must first drink a glass of sadness, and then a glass of gladness; the one in remembrance of the Queen's death, the other to the happy life of the King. When this cup of mortification went about, and every one like so many sextons, began to bury their dead, I could hardly forbear laughing to see such a set of sorrowful aspects. Had a stranger popped in at the instant, he could have expected no less than a second part of the counter-scuffle;[33] for they looked so very sour upon one another, as if they intended to turn the smoking joints into instruments of war, and were preparing rather to fight than feed. One cried, the drink, like the air, was bitter cold. Another

---

31 Literally 'workshop of the blood'. William Harvey had discovered the circulation of the blood in 1628.
32 i.e. 'insignificant persons' of the estate. (*OED*)
33 Presumably the war in Ireland when James II had attempted to regain the throne.

would have shuffled away his glass, saying, he had heard that Kings never die, and so he hoped the news was not true; but that would not pass. A third said, the drink was very dead, and he was never at such a sad funeral before, and prayed heartily that he might never live to see such another. To which a fourth who happened to be the parish clerk, shook his head, and in the bitterness of drink and spirit, cried Amen. In a word they all wished that the Queen had been alive, and that their sense of her loss had never been put to such a lamentable trial. And then they all unanimously pray, that the King might never die: but by their distorted ill-favoured faces I guessed they did not wish it so much for the King's sake as their own: they feared if the King should die, they should be again invited to the like sorrow, a dead, cold, and bitter draught.

But to raise their decayed spirits, sweeten their afflicted palates, and settle their trembling stomachs, the music played, the meat in a kind of revenge was vigorously dissected, and the King's health was often remembered in a sort of liquor that had more sweetness, life, and heat.

But Sir, though the King and the nation begin the new year with solemn mourning; yet, like my tragi-comic scene, I hope this sad beginning will have a jolly conclusion: may he fill the nation with his triumphs; may the French camp shrink at the sight of his purple, and swim in their own. And when he dies, may he leave a son who may continue his virtue, and inherit his great fame and fortune.

Which short rapture is not only the prayer, but perhaps the prophecy of

Sir

your faithful Servant,

W.L.

'a glass of sadness'

LETTER 47

INTRODUCTION

The Duke of Luxembourg has also died. Despite being a hunchback, he was one of the ablest of Louis XIV's generals – but the news does little to cheer Lawrence in his sadness at the Queen's death.

LETTER 47

For Sir Michael Hicks   January 5th 1694[5]

Sir,

You inform me how sad the City is without and within at the death of the Queen; the sorrow was begun but doth not dwell there; it spreads apace, and these remoter parts equally feel the loss and follow the example. The throne never was nor ever will be filled with so much virtue, nec primam visa est similem, nec habere sequentem [(she) seemed to have none, first or second, like her]. But death was never partial; he equally throws his dart at all, and is neither delayed by respect, nor softened by compassion: pauperum tabernas regumque turres [(death knocks at) the huts of the poor and the palaces of Kings].[34] The royal and the meaner virtues feel the same hasty fate, nor is there any security in birth and title. She seemed not only born to rule but to reform a corrupted age; some murmured at her life, but all suffer on her death.

Though her fate was not presaged by a comet,[35] yet it is followed by a terrible frost; what the heavens did not foretell, the earth feels: for upon the first news of the Queen's death, she began to cover her face and bury herself in snow; that whole inanimate body changed its complexion at the common loss, and hath looked white and pale ever since. But as colours are set off by contraries, and a young, plump, and beautiful Italian is attended by an old, lean, and deformed hag; so the Queen's virtuous youth, is followed by a vicious age, and the Duke of Luxembourg's death illustrates hers.[36] His deformity presaged desolation; he looked like a ruin, and laboured to turn everything into his own shape. But what nature bowed, death breaks: that small crooked body which while living raised such a dust, now dead makes

---

34 Horace, *Odes* 1.4, 13–14.

35 Bayle had published his *Miscellaneous Thoughts on the Comet of 1680* ' . . . wherein it is proved by several reasons drawn from philosophy and theology that comets are not presages of disaster'.

36 Lawrence has seemingly changed his opinion of Queen Mary: 'young, plump and beautiful' is more appreciative than one of a 'brace of fat does' of letter 24. Again he uses the word 'Italian' meaning 'with such characteristics' – perhaps comparing the Queen and Duke to characters from contemporary drama or literature.

less than another man; and he who commanded vast armies now takes up a narrower room than one of his common soldiers. I only wish he had fallen by the King's own hand, and not by God's immediate justice. I hear he died of a pleurisy; abundance of blood he shed, and by abundance of blood he died.

I am glad you have been long diverted by a society so agreeable and so nearly related; it is a happiness which I have out-lived, and am therefore forced to a life solitary and retired; I go but little abroad, and can be contented to sit so long as my eyes may have liberty to range. When I have a mind to look into the world, I only go into my commode and from that topping I can discover almost all that I desire to see. Among other remarkable objects I can see Pantly Court and a small hill in the County of Hereford; this latter upon the 12th of March 1571 was raised by an earthquake, and gently walking forward for two days together rested itself upon the higher ground.[37] The other was the place where the Countess of Pembroke formerly lived and where Sir Philip Sidney writ his Arcadia; there runs by it a little river called Leadon, which he likewise celebrates by that name, and in it bathes the bodies of his two royal beauties.[38]

But Sir, this untimely death of the Queen added to the sorrowful remembrance of my own private losses, makes me draw many a long sigh, and abruptly hasten to subscribe my self

Sir

your faithful Servant

W.L.

37 A contemporary account describes how 'Marclay Hill in the year 1575 after shaking and roaring for the space of three Days, to the great horror, fright, and Astonishment of the Neighbouring Inhabitants, began to move . . . ' (Fuller). It overthrew a chapel that stood on the hill, and altered the landscape over 20 acres. The hill, in the parish of Much Marcle, has since then been known as 'the Wonder'.

The explanation, not then understood, was that the phenomenon was caused by a landslip, not an earthquake. The sliding rocks pushed up the soil thus making it appear that the hill was rising.

All accounts give the year as 1575 except that of Sir Richard Baker (in his *Chronicle of the wonderful events in the reign of queen Elizabeth I*) who gave the year as 1571. Lawrence had obviously read this version.

38 'A sweet, now sweetest Ladon', said Zelmane, 'Why dost thou not stay thy course to have more full taste of thy happiness?' . . . etc; (Vol. 12 p. 179 of *Complete Works*, ed. E.A. Baker, Routledge).

The Countess of Pembroke was Sir Philip Sidney's sister, to whom he dedicated his *Arcadia*. The Leadon is a tributary of the Severn.

LETTER 48

INTRODUCTION

This is the second of two letters – both in the Appendix – in which Lawrence completes the description of the monuments and garden he is making at Shurdington. He writes of the ways in which he is trying to retain his memories for later generations. These letters, as well as the garden, would seem to be among such 'ways'.

LETTER 48

For Wm. Powlett Esqre;   [Undated]

Sir,

I formerly opened to you part of those monumental secrets into which my double loss, much sorrow, and a mourning fancy had engaged me. You ask now, what further progress I have made.

Sir, my eyes are not dry yet, and while they are running, I am sure my fancy can never stand still; every hour begets a new thought, and my sorrows find no end to their labours. When I saw how death had deprived me of all my nearest relations, had left me no wife, no issue living; no brother nor brother's son; no uncle nor uncle's son; nor any one that bore my own name, unless in remoter branches. And when I also saw by many examples that grief is never so strongly fixed in the mind but that time by degrees will insensibly dissolve and waste it, unless there be some outward objects to affect the sense, and help to continue the impression: I then turned my heavy thoughts into action, and grew so much in love with my own sorrow that I sought ways how I might meet it at every turn, and transmit the remembrance of it to the next age, when it had outlived mine. And yet I have so ordered the whole design, that to a stranger all the parts of it look very brisk and gay: they are only monuments to myself, and put no damp upon the spectator, or make him shrink at the sight of any thing that is either melancholy or mortal. But to satisfy your curiosity, you may tack the ensuing account to that which I formerly sent you . . . [see Appendix]

Sir, by this time I believe your curiosity grows uneasy, and you begin to repent of your enquiry: your great business puts a value upon your time, and every hour improves it. But mine lies upon my hands and I seek opportunities how to waste and consume it: of which perhaps this long account is not the least example. But however I have gratified your expectation, and opened the whole secret of my sorrows: for you being an alter idem [second self] my heart ought to lie in my hand: nothing is to be hid from the eyes of a friend, and just such is the unfeigned sincerity and freedom of

Sir,

Your most faithful friend and servant

W.L.

LETTER 49

For Dr Edward Browne   March 8th 1694/5

Sir,

I know your name is up [for election][39] and that you are much sought after by the distressed; you almost daily measure the lives of heirs and the length of families, a sort of threads that often break, and are as often broken. It is therefore true charity to the living to put you in mind of the dead, that a wary conscience may be your guide, and that if the patient must die, he may neither die deceived nor unprepared.

Perhaps you may think my grief intemperate; time seems to cure all wounds but mine: mine lies open all the year, but every 8th March makes it bleed afresh. If my son's danger was concealed because you did not know it, my sorrows are then rude and unjustly conveyed: but if you knew the danger, and therefore concealed it, my complaints are justly renewed, and I leave you to judge how far you are concerned, and how much you contributed to that fatal event, for you affirmed the security of life all along, and almost to the very point of death, which I had the faith and folly to believe against the opinion of many. But I will not give you their particular observations; I will neither enumerate nor upbraid. I only tell you that I have unhappily lost my peace and my posterity; so that my line being thus cut, and my name falling with my son, I may very aptly subscribe myself

Anonymous.

39 In 1694, Edward Browne was elected treasurer of the College of Physicians. He subsequently became President – from 1704 until his death in 1708. (*DNB*)

LETTER 50

INTRODUCTION

With no immediate heir (and no surviving near relations), Lawrence's remoter relations 'look with greedy wishes' on his estate. One such, perhaps, is Sir Thomas Lawrence and his wife, Anne, of Iver, in Buckinghamshire, and Chelsea. Lawrence and Sir Thomas have a nearer connection through Lawrence's younger uncle, Isaac, who is also Sir Thomas' uncle by marriage (see family tree, p. xii).

If the 'Sir Thomas' referred to in letter 45 is the Sir Thomas Lawrence of the following two letters, Lawrence has no liking for his wife – a type that 'has more bitterness than sweetness' – and on whom her husband has wasted his fortune. The latter is about to sail to Maryland, where he had previously held office as Secretary to the Council, leaving his wife and one of their sons at home.

Lawrence shows that he is not of the stuff of which Colonial pioneers were made.

LETTER 50

To the Lady Anne Lawrence   Oct. 6th 1695

Madam,

You gave me the honour of a letter and may very justly condemn me for not making a more speedy return of those many thanks which were due to so great an obligation. When I broke the seal, the first thing I looked upon was your name, which gave me a short surprise; for I thought that she who once writ the same fair hand and bore the same name, had gained the privilege of rising first, and had by that letter given me notice of her return to life. But it proved not more a sudden than a vain thought, for I see though we labour for precedence above ground, death allows none below, and though we sink at several times yet we must all rise at once.

Sir Thomas informs me that he is preparing for a second voyage, I am sorry he should leave a merry land for Mary-Land,[40] or that any minutes of his life should be destined to such a barbarous clime, where tobacco is the only current coin, and the whole salary must end in smoke.

Madam, you have been a liberal wife, and have brought him a fair treasure, it is too rich to be left and too good to be divided; and yet he tells me this latter is decreed, and he must sail away with one half. My cousin Thomas ('tis true) hath tried the danger and may venture again, especially

---

40 Maryland, named after Charles I's Queen, Henrietta Maria, was settled mainly as a refuge for English and Irish Roman Catholics – although its founder, Lord Baltimore, insisted on religious toleration.

having in revenge of his late captivity bombed and burnt St Malo.[41] But methinks my Cousin Harry is too tender for a winter voyage, and too smooth for a rough sea. You part with half your self and half your issue, and yet your condition like your merit exceeds mine: my whole family changed this world for another and return no more; while only one half of yours leave this world for the New, and may return again.

Madam, when Sir Thomas goes, I am sure your peace is gone as well as your person divided; but that all may end in a calm and that you may be once again not only happily, but inseparably united, shall be the often-repeated prayer of

Your most faithful Servant

W.L.

41 Young Thomas had accompanied his father to Maryland but returned earlier and had taken part in the war on the Continent. Thomas may have been taken prisoner during an attempted landing at Brest in June 1694 when about 500 men were killed or taken prisoner. (The French had known of the plan a month in advance.) The Navy bombarded the coastal ports of Northern France for the rest of that summer.

Alternatively, he may have been present at the bombardment of St Malo in November 1693, when a new 'infernal machine', a Dutch invention, was introduced which contained 'tar, sulphur, bitumen, nitre, and vitriol, with rows of grenades and barrels of powder'. It did some damage to St Malo – and killed the crew of the ship from which it was fired.

(*England in the Reign of James II and William III*, David Ogg, Oxford University Press, 1984).

LETTER 51

INTRODUCTION

Sir Thomas Lawrence (1645–1714) has also seen, or been given a description of, the gardens at Shurdington and has questioned their morbid association. Perhaps he hopes that one of his sons will one day inherit the estate.

LETTER 51

For Sir Thomas Lawrence [Bt.]   Oct. 6th 1695.

Sir,

In the length of your letter I see the strength of your reason; your patience and your parts are equally visible, the one in writing so much, the other in writing so well. But yet, as to my villa, I allow your sentiments, but cannot part with my own. 'Tis true, why should places of pleasure be crowded with emblems of grief and mortality? When we come to caress life we should perhaps lay aside all thoughts of death, and believe both our delights and ourselves to be immortal; for otherwise the enjoyment cools, the spirits grow faint and are repulsed in every sally. And

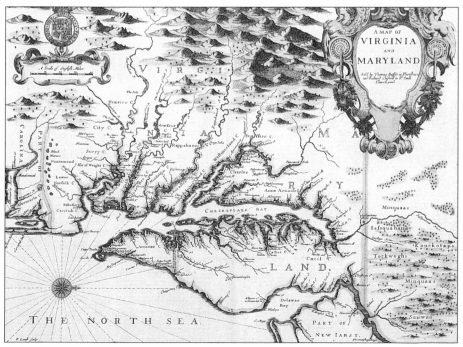

Virginia and Maryland in 1676

yet this is no new thing; the old Romans adorned their houses with the statues of their ancestors; and we in our parlours hang up the pictures of our deceased friends. Philip the 4th built his royal palace in the shape of a gridiron, and always ate, and walked, and slept, within that engine of martyrdom. Those remembrances were very legible and lay open to every eye; but mine are mihi tantum nota [known only to me], and the design appears not to the world, unless I turn the key and discover the secret.

Besides, my giving my pleasure this alloy of grief, is but joining the thistle to the rose, which is not mine but a royal mixture; King James first brought it out of Scotland when the two crowns were united; the sweet briar pleaseth the nose but pricks the fingers; while it obligeth one sense, it offends another. The noblest of our pleasures may win too much upon the heart, and make it cool to sublimer things, if there were nothing to check and curb it, in its career of vanity. The fancies of men are guided by their several passions, especially those of love and grief which, being more pleasing than the rest, we take the greater care to preserve and perpetuate. And yet I must tell you that time by degrees wears away the sharpness of the thought; that which was at first the design of a violent sorrow, is now turned to a pleasing remembrance and I take more delight in these melancholy fancies (partly because they are prima impressionis) than others can do in their highest and best enjoyments.

I am sorry your unexpected business not only stopped your intended visit, but invites you again to Mary-land;[42] where your gain cannot equal your loss, nor the profits you expect make satisfaction for the comforts you forsake: you sail to the West Indies[43] and leave the East Indies at home, you leave an orient pearl and diamonds which all love for a sorry weed [tobacco] which many hate, you go to a place where trade is not managed by money

---

42 Sir Thomas had first gone to Maryland as a 'royal placeman' and became Secretary (and for a time, President) of the Council. His hopes of acquiring a fortune were disappointed when he found that his salary had been appropriated to government needs. For demanding a share in the salary of the employees of the office in lieu, he was tried and imprisoned for 6 months in 1692 but was reinstated by the King. His return to England was, presumably, to sort out the vexed question of his salary. In 1698, Sir Thomas resigned in favour of his son, Thomas, but returned again to Maryland for 4–5 years after young Thomas died of fever in 1707.

Sir Thomas died in 1714 and is buried in Chelsea Old Church. A modern kneeler in the church, embroidered with the arms of Maryland, commemorates his association with the State.

The Lawrence chapel in Chelsea Old Church (almost the only part to survive its destruction in the Second World War) contains a number of tombs of this branch of the family, including that of Sir Thomas' grandmother, Lady Grizel, who had a 'patent for eternity' (letter 18).

(*His Lordship's Patronage. Offices of Profit in Colonial Maryland*, D. MacClure Owings, Baltimore, Maryland Historical Society. And Burke's *Extinct and Dormant Baronetcies*.)

43 The trading and customs area of the Southern District extended from Maryland and Virginia to the West Indies.

but wars, where people exchange goods for goods, and rather barter than buy: where hoops are used instead of locks, and their treasure is kept not in chests but hogsheads; and where the sentence upon our last dissolution is divided, the man only falls to dust, and his wealth to ashes.

Sir, I shall be very glad to hear from you before you embark, however if your departure be speedy, my best wishes shall sail along with you; and that you may go safe and return rich shall be always inserted in the most devout petitions of

Sir

Your faithful Servant and Kinsman

W.L.

LETTER 52

INTRODUCTION

Another distant cousin has asked Lawrence to stand godfather to his child, an infant William Lawrence. Perhaps this cousin, too, has his eye on Shurdington.

LETTER 52

To my Cousin R. Lawrence   Oct. 1. 1695.

Sir,

Your letter invites me to the font; the making of Christians is a noble work, and a cheap; 'tis but a few words and a few drops, and the business is done. I am sorry I cannot give the parson my personal security. For I allow an attorney in matters of law but not of religion; these sacred rites, this possession of grace should be delivered propria persona. But since this cannot be, I have provided a proxy, who I think will come very near your other two sureties in age, merit, and fortune.

The Jacobites like their founder are things of little courage and shallow sense, and therefore I am well pleased that you intend to make the infant a Williamite, but I hope it is not for my sake but the King's; for methinks those who bear his name, and happen to be born under the influence of such a bright and active planet, must share in his felicity and greatness of mind. And therefore I may well expect that your content in this new birth will grow up with his years, and that as he riseth in age and proportion, he may also thrive in all the ornaments of nature and fortune, and live long and happy. And if those of your posterity who are yet to come, will follow the example, I may then justly wish that you may get children in saecula saeculorum, that is, that you yourself may oblige this age, your sons the next, and so on to the last period of time.

These few wishes contain mighty things, and need no other addition of words from

Sir,

Your affectionate Cousin

W.L.

LETTER 53

INTRODUCTION

The mantle of Uncle William has fallen on Lawrence. A furious letter to Captain William — (a young cousin?) follows. A youthful Lawrence had written to his friend 'W.H.' (letter 4) and complained that the older generation 'have the purse and the power to back their opinion, and therefore claim it as their right to judge and decree as they please . . . '. Captain William's offences, nevertheless, seem more extreme than Lawrence's had been at a similar age. The uncharacteristic mixing of metaphors suggests the extent of Lawrence's outrage – but then it was the revered King William whom the Captain had failed to support.

LETTER 53

[To Captain William —]   [Undated]

Sir,

I have put your letter upon the same pile with the rest, that if anyone shall have a mind to study civility and eloquence, he may resort to those useful records for instruction. I verily believe that an ingenious man before he would have answered so many silly letters upon such a sorry concern, would rather wish to have rowed in a galley, or have lived under one of the ten persecutions. That honour of yours which you so often mention seems to me but a rough, rude and misshapen lump. You would do well to lick it into better form; and yet when you have done as much as you can I doubt it will be but the cub of a bear still. . . .

If I had dabbled away a whole active Summer at the Bath, if I had declined the bullets to follow the bowls, left the hazard and chance of war for those upon the dice; and lazily taken in the French claret, while others were lustily letting out the French blood; I should have e'en nailed my blushing engrailéd cross to some post for men to deride and dogs to piss upon.[44]

William the King rushed boldly per mare per terras into all the dangers of Cannae while William the Captain by a more wary conduct sheltered himself among the delights of Capua.[45] When a war-like passion should have swelled him in the King's camp, he was softly melting himself away in the King's bath: which I think is such a stain to your pretended honour that all those hot springs can never wash away. . . .

44 The Lawrence coat of arms was a red cross, (Argent, a cross raguly gules). Lawrence points to his 'engrailéd cross' in his portrait on p. ii (see also p. 82).
45 Cannae was the site of Hannibal's famous victory against the might of Rome; Capua the city whose enervating climate subsequently wrought havoc on the morale of Hannibal's army.

LETTER 54

INTRODUCTION

In this letter, Lawrence admits that he has been ill – which may account for a renewed irascibility. It is not, however, only for this reason that he is relieved that he will not be selected as High Sheriff for Gloucestershire. As he wrote in a letter to Sir Michael Hicks on 17th November: ' . . . I quietly wear out my short remains of life in my own villa without either envy or emulation, . . . to know myself and enjoy my friends is the greatest prudence of a declining age, and the only useful enjoyment that is now prized and sought by Sir, your faithful Servant
W.L.'

LETTER 54

For Wm. Powlett, Sergeant at Law   December 4th 1695

Sir,

You assure me that I am none of the three [nominees], and so I conclude that the danger of being High Sheriff is over for this year; however I thank you for your care to observe it, and your resolution to prevent it.[46] For, this distemper which I had and whose return I often fear, confines me still to a strict moderation in drink and diet; and unless I would break those as yet necessary rules, I could neither go on with security nor come off with reputation.

There is nothing to be got by that office and all people avoid it, but to be a Burgess or a Knight of the Shire stirs up the ambition of the great; to be one among five hundred is such a charming honour, that the candidates bid high and buy at any rate, they spare no money nor pains to procure it, and the common sort promote the party they take with so much heat as if they were fighting pro aris et focis [for their altars and hearths]. Sir J. [Sir John Guise Bt., Whig] and Mr S. [Thomas Stephens, Tory] labour hard in the body and Mr B. [not identified] in the borders: so that the whole County is in a ferment.[47] The brains and the barrels have been long working for voices.

---

46 The position of High Sheriff was much more onerous then than now – many of the High Sheriff's responsibilities having since been taken over by the Police.

47 The increased business of the Nation had produced a proliferation of places and pensions for the ambitious M.P. so that the dying Sir John Guise (2nd Bart) tried to nominate his 18 year-old son to succeed him.

The Gloucestershire candidates were not alone in using bribery to influence the voters. After this election, one Whig candidate (a Mr Mayne of Aylesbury) had complained of irregularities in the poll. In the resulting House of Commons hearing, one man said he had been told that 'what drink they drew for Mr Herbert' (the Tory candidate) 'they should be paid for'. ' . . . And Susan Dunscombe said, Edward Edwards voted for Mr Herbert, because he had given him a black pig.'

(*House of Commons Journals* XII, pp. 417–19)

When the tubs are full they make but a dead sound, but as they sink the voice rises: by Wednesday next they will be all drawn to a stoop and then the whoops will begin. And I believe many a freeholder would burst if the wind in their heads and their lungs had not some vent in the bung.

Sir M. [Hicks?] tells me that he sees you often, but sure it must be by candle-light, for they talk here of such great fogs at London that you can hardly see one another: and a neighbour of mine having lately some business near that city went thither to see it, but after he had groped in the fog 5 days, his patience was quite worn out, and he came away as wise as he went. You may have more society but we have more light. Sir M. enjoys that which I covet; I much desire your conversation and his,[48] but know not how to break through the impediment of deep roads and short days.

When I tell you that Christmas is hard by, I have told you all the diversion that I am to expect here; and when I also tell you that this great festival will afford me but a sorry satisfaction, for it chiefly consists in stuffing the carcases of rational brutes, I am sure we shall not differ in opinion.

But, Sir, I shall waste no more of your time than what is wrapped up in this short assurance, that though your health and happiness may (like our triumvirs)[49] have many voices, yet none shall be more freely given or more often repeated than that of Sir,

Your faithful Servant

W.L.

'You may have more society but we have
more light'

48 Only one letter from Sir Michael Hicks is known to exist (written to his brother on parish matters) which opens with an image of conviviality: 'Sir, Being taking a bottle with Mr John Hill the last night . . . ' (*A Cotswold Family*).
49 i.e. the prospective Members of Parliament.

LETTER 55

INTRODUCTION

On the 4th anniversary of Willy's death, Lawrence again wrote to Edward Browne. The message is the same but a different emphasis emerges when Lawrence apportions some of the blame to himself: 'That which often sharpens my grief, and makes my oversight as afflicting as yours was fatal, is this, he [Willy] began from some outward symptoms to suspect that your potions had in 'um too much of the Jesuit [bark], and desired the opinion of some other physician and which, upon your positive and often repeated assurance of the truth of his pulse and that he was past all danger, was by me unhappily neglected'.

If anything, the letter is crueller than the rest. He continues: 'When a gross mistake is committed, the sin to conceal is certainly greater than the shame to confess; and if anyone suffers a life to be thus wilfully lost, the guilt is of a bloody die, and there wants only the addition of malice to make it murder'.

Edward Browne can take no more and shows the letter to his sister, Anne Fairfax – to whom (in letters 28–30) Lawrence had first written of both Anne's and Willy's deaths.

LETTER 55

For Madam Anne Fairfax   March 20th 1695/6

Madam,

In the annual remembrance which I sent to your brother, I only opened my own thoughts, but have at no time offered to disturb yours. Yet since you have casually known that which was directed to him alone, and which for your sake I designed to be a secret: be your resentments either from reason or nature, they have charmed me to a future silence, and I shall strike no more upon that rock. I will hereafter shut up my sorrows, and they shall rather tear my own breast, than afflict yours. You may see in this the great extent of your power, you can give limits to the rights of nature, and can subdue other's passions as well as command your own.[50]

---

50 Anne had been widowed the previous year and had, herself, lost several children in infancy. There is a touching tablet in Hurst Parish Church 'Dedicated to ye Memory of William Fairfax son to Henry Fairfax Esq; by Anne his Wife daughter to Sir Thomas Browne Kt', who had died in 1684, just after his second birthday:

'This little, silent, gloomy Monument
Contains all that was sweet and Inocent. . . . '

After an earlier baby had died in 1680, Sir Thomas Browne had written to Edward Browne (Sept 15th 1680): ' . . . my daughter Fairfax, who though shee hath had many occasions to learne

I very well know your brother's modesty and merit; I know his reputation and his learning are equally wide, but being well assured, and that by judgements more solid and piercing than my own, that there was some great if not gross mistake in the case of my son: the sense of that untimely and terrible loss made me take that liberty which perhaps is not commonly practised, and which indeed, if I had not as well sought the security of other families as deplored the ruin of my own, had been a very insipid and vain relief.

My philosophy (as you term it) might in a meaner concern have been sufficient either to have wasted or weakened my sorrows, and though I have no will to justify where you think you have reason to complain, yet, Madam, I must tell you, I have lost a son, and an only son, a youth shaped within and without to the height of my wishes. The matrimonial links when broken may be easily tacked together again by a new choice: but as for another son, it is too late to seek and too long to rear. I have lost my posterity; and in that, the only prudent end of marriage, which is to leave one behind us who may represent and inherit. In a word, I have lost all, and the felicity of my life is extinguished.

Upon the more solid and religious thoughts, I know names and families are but vain things; but if we should drive from our minds every thing that is vain, the business of life is over and we must have done thinking. For the whole stage of this world and all its painted scenes are only thin superficial shows, and nothing else but vanity in various shapes. . . .

And thus, Madam, you see how in all points I aim at your peace, and I shall never think myself more happy than when I can either serve or obey, and show to the utmost of my ability how much I am

Dear Madam,

Your faithful Servant,

W.L.

---

patience, hath I feare not sufficiently [w]ayghed and prepared her thoughts agaynst the uncertaintie of things, and yet I like that temper better than to bee sad for nothing, as long as they are well themselves, as is the manner of voluptuous and sensuall persons'.

If Anne now preaches patience to Lawrence, it is from a knowledge born of all too many examples of the 'uncertaintie of things'.

(*The Works of Sir Thomas Browne*, Vol IV. ed. Geoffrey Keynes, Faber and Faber; also Hurst Parish registers. The poem on William Fairfax's memorial tablet is quoted in Aphra Behn's edited *Miscellany, being a collection of poems by several Hands . . .* – although it is unattributed.)

LETTER 56

INTRODUCTION

Lawrence has been ill again and sought medical advice. Dr John Radcliffe (1650–1714) became the most sought-after doctor of his day – although frequently consulted more for the enjoyment of his wit than for his medical skill. He had the reputation of being a heavy drinker, which gives a curious ring to his recommendation to Lawrence to drink only water. Water was seldom drunk in the seventeenth century so the suggestion is, in fact, unusual. On at least one occasion (the death-bed of the poet Earl of Rochester, in 1680) Dr Radcliffe had been assisted by Dr Edward Browne.

There is a reference to the new minted coinage which had just been issued to replace the old stamped money. The exchange had been made too rapidly and, for a time, there was an acute shortage of money in circulation – resulting in a good deal of hardship and discontent.

LETTER 56

For William Powlett. Sergeant at Law.   Nov. 26th 1696

Sir,

You tell me that the report of two unusual things, that is, my going to London in haste and in my own coach gave you a great suspicion of my being ill; nor did you err in your conjecture, for I went not to see the city but to save myself.

Dr Radcliffe had left some remains of my lurking fever; he had only covered but not extinguished the fire; for, growing stronger by degrees, it at last emptied and inflamed all the muscular parts: my tongue was so scorched and as it were, charked[51] by this inward heat, that it was almost as black and dry as a cinder. My memory was woefully battered, I had an uneven motion, and some convulsions in the nerves; so that being very weak and wasted I declined the sociable part of the town, and was resolved to lie incognito till I was well assured of my fate. But the danger is now over, and I thank you for searching after me with so much care and concern.

But this one thing I often remember when I was at the weakest, and my spirits so very low that they seemed to be taking leave of their old acquaintance, I had so much quiet, and so profound a calm within, that the thought of all my temporal concerns was quite vanished, and I could have died with content. Which made me observe, that in ipso limine mortis [on the very threshold of death], it is only the quantity of spirits which struggle so hard for life and so strongly oppose a dissolution.

If I get home time enough to the venison you design for me at Christmas, my friends shall be treated with it on New Year's day by their new

---

51 'Charcoal' derives from the same word.

neighbour. I may well call myself so, for the old man is quite put off; all my former flesh is slipped away from the skin and the bone, and that little which I wear about me is perfectly new. And that I may be all of a piece, I have turned my old dress and my old hair into a brighter colour; I have put on a new youthful habit, a full wig, and an Indian gown so well inhabited with various figures, that were it not for the foreign dress, you would think, when I walked, that the whole parish was in motion. So that when you see me, you will probably search for your old friend; you can take me for no less than another thing and a graver[52] sort of Beau. For by this change in body and habit, all the old materials, like our old hammered money, seem to be called in, refined, and new-stamped: so that I appear even to myself to be new coined, and, as if I were just brought out of the mint, I look as brisk and bright as our new money. There remains only this one thing imperfect, densae occulos pressere tenebrae [thick shadows pressed upon (my) eyes].[53] My eyes are at present so weak that I am fain to support 'um with a new pair; but these shades being gathered only by the sleepy draughts which I take every night, will (by my former experience) soon break away and clear those obstructed lights.

In the mean time I continue to drink water; long use hath given that element a good relish and esteem which I formerly thought had none. As I wish you, so I allow you to be the happier man; you drink it for pleasure, but I by advice. The subjects if they will follow my example can never swallow water in a better time; for though they want money and complain with much heat, yet they may have drink enough and such as will cool their discontented lungs.

As to your enquiry into the reasons of the late vote for calling in all the hammered money; this might be one and the greatest, that the suppressing all the remains of the old coin would prevent the hoarding up of the new; and that there would be no curiosity where there were no distinction. And so when one piece of silver came to be no better esteemed than another, the money would circulate with more ease, and the whole treasure of the Nation would be always in motion.

Thus, Sir, for want of better intelligence, I have entertained you with the news of myself, and this the rather, because while I tell you that the shadow of the dial is set back, I may also tell you, that my life receives this addition of days with the greater content, since I gain thereby both more strength and a longer time to show to the world and you how much I am

Sir,

Your faithful Servant

W.L.

---

52 As of a ship's hull, cleaned and re-tarred while in a 'graving dock'.
53 Lucan, *Civil War* 7, 616.

LETTER 57

INTRODUCTION

Two months later, Lawrence has again been away but, before returning home, writes briefly to Sir Michael Hicks of 'pros and cons', of more than Gordian knots – and even turns to verse. He is being deliberately obscure.

LETTER 57

For Sir Mich: Hicks   January 5th 1696/7

Sir,
Since nothing ought to be hid from the best of my friends, I will not leave this city 'til I have drawn the curtain and discovered a secret against which I have so often and so openly declared.

Fatis agimur, cedite Fatis.
[We are driven by the Fates – yield to them.]

See the irresistible powĕr of fate,
I draw in that yoak which I always did hate.
Love, youth, and ambition have long left the stage
And all things give way to the prudence of age.

For in a full council of thoughts this matter was heard and re-heard, often and fairly argued pro and con: 'til at last, a solid and impartial reason, which in mine and all other cases is the best of judges, having summed up the arguments on both sides, was clear of opinion. That I should tie a knot, which beyond that of Gordius, can neither be untied nor cut: and which (though in dark expressions) is now opened to you by

                    Sir,

                         Your faithful Servant

                              Wm. Lawrence.

LETTER 58

One (un-named) friend objects to the betrayal of principle, but Sir Michael Hicks – and the local bell-ringers – have greeted the news contained in the last letter with 'much real content'. In an age (and by a man) much concerned with anniversaries, it can be no accident that the following letter is written on January 12th – the anniversary of Anne's death.

Lawrence argues his case very much like the lawyer he was trained to be.

LETTER 58

For Sir Michael Hicks   January 12th 1696/7

Sir,

You received the late obscure intimation of the change of my condition with so much real content, and so many kind words and wishes, that I can do no less than acknowledge it to be a just addition to those many favours which I have so often received, and you so liberally bestowed.

But — (perhaps by reason of an expectation probably lost) seems to upbraid me with the breach of resolution. He being an old bachelor did always inveigh against marriage, and I, thinking it to be a great addition to the cares of life, did also openly resolve to decline it. And though I am fallen from the confederacy, yet in him it had been much more civil and obliging rather to cover, than to complain, or seem willing to have tied a friend to such a rambling resolution. For admit there was then a fieri non debet [it should not happen], yet there is now an irrevocable factum est [fait accompli]: and he might well have seen that my declining constitution did justly invite me to look out for those means which were most proper to support it. You know how fast he clings to his own ipse dixit [dogmatic statement based on bare authority], and is himself guilty of one sort of marriage, that is, he is so wedded to his own opinion, that he thinks the strength of his particular reason (like the unreasonable power of a single Polander) to be sufficient to suspend or break the debates of a whole Diet.[54]

But excluding his opinion, I followed my own, and complied with the common desire and expectation. For perhaps few matches of our rank were ever consummate with a more general satisfaction. For her obliging nature, her first and true quality, and the wrongs of fortune were so well known in this country, that all the neighbourhood rejoiced at the union, and this parish made the bells publish the reality of their wishes by the free gift of two

---

54 In the Polish Seym, all votes had to be unaminous, and any one deputy could defeat a motion by saying 'I object'.

whole days ringing. (The same person, as a deeper stroke of mortification, acquaints me with this Italian saying, when an elderly man embraces a woman, he embraces death: but I told him, that proverb was levelled at old fond fools who married young and buxom ladies whose constitution required more than the security of life could spare; and that there was in the same language another saying, pian piano, soft and fair; and I should be sure to take care of the main chance, and keep my calmer spirits from such wild expense.) For I was not driven to this change by a brutal impulse; my resolution was guided by more lofty thoughts: I long used the scales of deliberation, and, (as I thought) weighed every thing by the balance of sound and solid reason.[55]

But Sir, to pass this, it hath been long my opinion, that I am not only accountable to God, but to my friend for all my actions of the greater moment, and therefore after the single combat between the pro and the con was ended, in which the latter made but a faint resistance and was easily disarmed, I digested my thoughts into the following method, that you might see, the change of my condition, and the choice of the person was not a rash act, but a resolution built not only upon sound reason, but upon a long and solid debate.

The question was, whether I should marry again? And if so, then to whom, and how qualified: that is, what harbour I should seek, and what rocks I should avoid. As to the former, it was always my opinion, that when a man parts with his liberty, he not only enters into the bonds but into the bondage of marriage: for by confining himself unto certain duties (the debita jura tori [the required duties of the bed]) he lives as it were in a prison; and if at any time he steals out of the rules and endeavours to make an escape, he must know that the curtains hang upon rods, and he is sure at night to hear the sad noise of his shackles. But to oppose this opinion, time hath brought in new reasons, and new reasons bring in new resolutions.

My long line expired with my son, my brother and both my uncles died, as I now live, without issue. So that every day closed in a deep melancholy: and wanting that society wherewith I used to wear away the long solitary nights, I seemed in my expiring years to be like Adam in his first hours, naked and alone. I saw that my health did much decay, and my years increase; the one requiring care; and the other, ease. For though my soul was naturally and almost always in a perfect calm, yet the common affairs of life, having a frequent influence upon the passions, these would sometimes ruffle

---

55 There is no certain clue to the identity of the 'old bachelor' who opposed Lawrence's remarriage. Lawrence is obviously distressed by the criticism, which suggests it is a friend, or relation, who is close to him. The suspicion that it could be William Powlett persists. (The lost 'expectation' could refer to his possible plan to retire to Shurdington – letter 41.)

and shake its serene temper. I also considered that death having cut off all my nearest relations, I lay open to the expectation of remoter kindred. The eyes of almost the whole tribe make strict enquiries into my inclinations, look with greedy wishes upon my estate, and were ready to invade the possession. I also observed that in a married life though there was less liberty, yet there was a greater reputation: and that among the nuptial birds, they who married with prudence did generally look brisk and sing in their cages. I saw such men did always approve of matrimony; but all the women did not only applaud but adore it. They did so much dote upon that condition of life, and laboured so hard to unite the two sexes, that they would allow no friendship between male and female unless it passed the seal of marriage, and till then they would either deride or suspect the virtue of a single life.

For these reasons, and after a pause of some years, I thought it convenient to marry again. But then, qualis futura sit uxor [what sort of wife I would have][56] was my great doubt and enquiry. For the nature of that sex is so much a riddle, so intricate, and so full of turnings and windings, that our liberty must not be hastily resigned; it requires a sharp eye and a long observation.

And therefore as to the other part of the question: my more mature thoughts upon the consideration of my advanced years resolved to avoid three things, youth, beauty, and fortune. The two former as inconsistent with my age: the latter with my ease, and all three whether single or united, likely to subdue the freedom of my life, and enter me into a slavish yoke.

Not youth; for, non sum qualis eram [I am not as I was].[57] I much differ from my former years. When the sun draws near the West, his heat grows cool and infirm. Horace, sensible of his own decay, was very earnest in his prayer to Venus when he said, parce precor, precor; desine circa lustra decem flectere mollibus jam durum imperiis [spare me, I pray, I pray; cease to guide with your soft commands one who is near fifty and now stiff].[58] Some aged men will vainly boast of their abilities; but he modestly confessed, that the expectation of a young lady was not to be gratified with the slow and faint addresses of a man of fifty.

Not beauty; for, that is the vanity of vanities. Every day threatens it: every sickness either lessens or breaks it. And though the poets resemble a fair face to roses and lilies, floribus almae lilia mista genae [lilies mingled with the

---

56 Juvenal, *Satires* 10, 353.
57 Horace, *Odes* 4, 1.3.
58 A partial quotation from Horace, *Odes* 4, 1, 2–7.

flowers of a gracious cheek]; yet it was not more for the fine complexion, than the short existence, *perdit spina rosas, nec semper lilia candent* [the thorn spoils the roses, and lilies do not flower for ever].[59] Such a superficies is too thin for a solid judgment; such nets may catch young birds: but the gravity of age must not be tempted with the levity of such gaudy colours.

Not fortune; for, if it be in land: I must be troubled with that vexatious addition, whereas in truth wanting a *terminus ad quem* [terminating point], that is, a son to inherit, I have stopped the course of my ambition. My former desire of heaping Pelion upon Ossa, earth upon earth, is now so wasted that I have been long weary of my own.[60] If it be in money, a small sum I despise, a great one I fear. For I must by a very liberal jointure have made satisfaction for my numerous years; and by the late but odd mode of settlement, which gives up the right to feoffees, and secures the inheritance to the tenth son before the first is begun, I shall cut off my disposing power, and by her long life after mine either stop or hazard the execution of a long design.[61] He who upon such a light reason, and by so weak an act, brings an infinite or at least unlimited extent into the narrow bounds of his single life thus murders his own disposing liberty, is a kind of *felo de se* [self-murderer], and when his hands are thus fast and foolishly tied, methinks he looks little better than a convicted felon.

But if our aged spark happens to meet with all these three, they grow as dreadful as the three points of Jupiter's thunderbolt. He falls into a certain slavery, and then *actum est de vetulo et vitulo* [the old man and the young heifer are done for], there's an end of an old fool. For at night their faces like those of Janus, will quickly look two ways.[62] The young lady sighs, and the old man coughs: she turns one way, and he, another. They lie in bed like the letter ∞, and join only in the brawny part. He may sometimes offer to lay three to one, but he can very seldom stand to his wager. Till at last his declining ability makes him totally despised, and the man usually becomes a monster; gaining (by a very sorry sort of exchange) that strength above, which he had lost below. Besides a lady thus qualified may not be gained but by much time and submission. The aged man must seem to be all on fire; must vainly boast of the return of youth and vigour; must put on many

---

59 Ovid, cf. *Art of Love*, 2, 115f.

60 When the Giants attempted to climb to Heaven, they placed Mt Pelion on Mt Ossa – two peaks in Thessaly – to form a mounting block.

61 Lawrence's problem seems to have been that, in marrying a young wife, he would have to make a generous settlement, probably by mortgaging his land. He might still hope for another son but, when making a Will, would want to leave Shurdington to his wife for her lifetime but, if there were no heir, would wish the estate to revert to a member of his family (i.e. the feoffees – those to whom the estate was to be conveyed) on her death. Unless he made his wife's inheritance conditional on her not marrying again, she could, by law, leave it to whomsoever she wished, including the family of a second husband.

62 The double-faced Roman God who, looking both ways, kept the Gates of Heaven.

amorous postures; look like a languishing fool and perhaps live two or three months in this slavish disguise. Her consent, (for love there can be none) must be purchased with bright temptation of pearl and diamonds; time must be fettered to her side in a golden chain; and large glittering lockets must adorn her breast and her buttock. She must every day spend some hours in reforming the supposed defects of nature by a tedious dress, she must have her washes, and place her numerous patches with judgment and order. Upon which sorry additions the aged consort must gaze and admire, though they are never designed for his weak eyes, but for the young and the gay.

Having shifted the servants, and taken in a set of new faces, she then claims an exclusive right in the coach, sends her single command to have it got ready, that she may dine with this or that modish lady; which done the several visits must be returned in form. And thus this young beauty is very often upon the ramble; the high-trotters on one side or other and always in motion; and so the old man's house is almost daily filled with noise and smoke. Which in my case would utterly break that retirement which I have so long sought and enjoyed; and of which the misfortunes of my family have made me resolutely fond. Besides this, she would never endure to hear me praise the virtue, beauty, great wit, and fidelity of her predecessor; she would hate, and perhaps deface those monuments, which I have raised to her memory; and when I was safe within the jurisdiction of the curtain and

'she must have her washes and place her numerous patches'

the rod, she would call me to an account for owning my first love, and chide me out of my mourning fancies.

It is true, when I was young, my judgment went along with the common opinion; I thought in marriage, as in arms, argent and or were the best metals, and had the brightest and most tempting complexions. But time hath worn off those thoughts, my misfortunes have stifled that covetous ambition and my age makes me warily firm against the dangerous enchantment of too much youth and beauty. I say, my age: for though as yet I have not all the signs of winter: five of my six senses are young enough; and my head is neither covered, nor my hair interlined with snow. Yet when I number my years, I find myself so near a borderer upon that cold and frozen quarter, that time will quickly make me an old man, and enter me into that infirm and condemned list.

Having thus cut through the opposing waves and not only discovered but declined the rocks, I have at last reached a secure harbour; a harbour free from those suspected storms, and full of ease and content; which was the happy life I sought. But that my reputation, of which I am as nice as an ermine of his skin, may not seem to be stained with the least spot of imprudence, I will tell you whom and what I have chosen. Her name is Dulcibella; she is finely shaped, and very genteel both in habit and humour. She is dressed in a minute; spends very little time at the glass, and her only business is mine. So that, as is intimated in part of her name, she is curarum dulce levamen [a sweet consolation for worries];[63] which swells her small fortune, and is a portion in itself. Her very obliging behaviour both to the rich and the poor gained her the good word and the good wishes of all. She is a very good gentlewoman, not only by the father, grandfather and ten descents beyond him: but by the mother, grandmother, great grandmother &c.[64] She is head of her name and family. She was born co-heir to at least £1500 an: in the parish of Witney, and so continued till the estate was imprudently wasted. Part of which, called Witney Farm of £1000 an: consisting of two parks, 12 groves, rich meadows and a fine river, was so fitted for the genteel recreations of hunting, fowling and fishing, that King Charles the first would often say, it was the best farm in England.[65] Besides this, by the provision of Sir Thomas White, (the

---

63 cf. Martial *Epigrams* 6.68.5.

64 Dulcibella's father's family were the Wisemans of Sparsholt Court, West Hendred, in Berkshire. Her mother's family were the Dunches of Pusey in Oxfordshire. A Mr Dunch of Pusey (Dulcibella's grandfather or uncle, perhaps) has come down in history as a parliamentary candidate for Abingdon, in September 1679. His supporters, including 100 mounted and 200 on foot, marched through the town, crying 'a Dunch, a Dunch', after he had gained most votes – but seen his opponent returned by the Mayor.

65 Dulcibella's connection with Witney Park is elusive. It is just possible that it could have been through the Brise (or Brice) family of Witney, themselves connected by marriage to the Yates family, owners of Witney Park before the Civil War.

Founder of St John's College and Merchant Taylor's schools, and to whom she is first kinswoman) all her sons (if she shall have any) are provided for.[66]

   This person whom I have thus described, and which to a generous nature is an eternal obligation, I have redeemed from the injustice of her ancestors and the wrongs of fortune. The life of a Plebeian was lightly regarded by the Roman senate; but their care was so great for men of their own quality, that he who saved a citizen or gentleman of Rome had the thanks of the Republic, and was honoured with a civic crown. So that upon a full view of all my circumstances I think the choice I have made is much to my profit and advantage: and if so, then I have gained a great and celebrated point: for omne punctum qui miscuit utile dulci [he wins every vote who mixes the useful with the sweet].[67]

viz: Dulcibella.

POST-SCRIPT TO LETTER 58

The life of 'ease and content' which Lawrence had so earnestly sought was short-lived – and he probably never fully regained his health. In the last letter in the manuscript, written in the early months of 1696/7, he thanks a cousin for his visit and hopes to return that visit when the days are warmer. He died in August that year, at the age of 60 or 61, and was buried beside Anne and Willy in Badgeworth Church. The lettering on the stone, in the north aisle, though much worn, is still just discernible. (That of William Lawrence, senior, a few feet away, is more easily legible).

   He had made his Will[68] in April, 'being by many examples sensible of the uncertainty of life and . . . so I may with more peace finish this life and with more vigour prepare and fit my soul for that . . . '. Dulcibella was to have the house for life with trustees appointed to administer the estate. She was to receive the majority of the income from the rents and provision was also made for Lawrence's sister, Jane Wright. There were detailed instructions for the maintenance of a son which 'shall be born either at the time of my death or after . . . ' (it does not seem to have occurred to him that he might have a daughter) but no such son was born. Dulcibella's legacy included 'my plate and

66 Sir Thomas White (1492–1567) was a merchant, Master of the Merchant Taylor's Company and Lord Mayor of London in 1553. His foundation of St John's College, Oxford, and assistance in founding the Merchant Taylor's School (the main founder was Richard Hilles), and many other charities, left him a poor man at the end of his life. He left no children. (*DNB*)
67 Horace, *The Art of Poetry*, 343.
68 Public Record Office, PROB 11/444, Folio 57.

jewels and the inlaid cabinet which stands in the chamber where I now lie . . . '. The description suggests this might be a Dutch marquetry cabinet of the kind made popular at the time by William and Mary. She was also to have 'my coach and horses, my wagon carts, cattle and sheep'. She did not remarry.

Failing a son, Shurdington was to go, after Dulcibella's death, to one of a list of Lawrence cousins and their heirs. The first name on the list was Lawrence's godson, William Lawrence (see letter 52). Of the seven names on the list, five had died without living heirs by the time of Dulcibella's death, forty years later, in 1736. The sixth, Littleton Lawrence, second son of Robert Lawrence of Cricklade, inherited the estate.

Several servants were to be given payments and annuities, in amounts varying from £5–£50. The names do not include a 'Ned' so, if he was a member of the household, he must, it seems, have died of the gout (see letters 39 & 42).

To Sir Michael Hicks, he left 'my blue sapphire ring which I desire him to wear for my sake'; two silver bowls were to be engraved and given to Trinity College, Oxford, in memory of Willy.

Lawrence, in fact, copied the affectionate and grateful letter (No 56) to William Powlett into his letter-book *after* the letter to Sir Michael Hicks, announcing his marriage. If Judge Powlett was indeed the 'old bachelor' who, with prophetic reasoning, objected to Lawrence's remarriage, this may suggest the spirit, if not yet the fact, of reconciliation.

The Lawrence family remained at Shurdington for a further 150 years.

DULCIBELLA'S FAMILY TREE

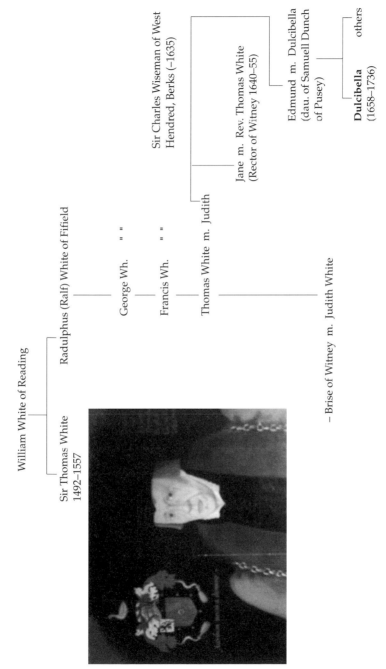

William White of Reading
—— Radulphus (Ralf) White of Fifield

Sir Thomas White
1492–1557

George Wh.   " "

Francis Wh.   " "

Thomas White m. Judith

Sir Charles Wiseman of West
Hendred, Berks (–1635)

Jane m. Rev. Thomas White
(Rector of Witney 1640–55)

Edmund m. Dulcibella
(dau. of Samuell Dunch
of Pusey)

Dulcibella
(1658–1736)

others

— Brise of Witney m. Judith White

Compiled from *The Visitations of Berkshire*, Harleian Society, 1907, Vol 1, Parish Registers.

Appendix A

The two parts of this appendix were written for William Powlett and describe the garden, at Shurdington, which Lawrence designed in memory of five generations of his family. The gardens themselves were drawn by Johannes Kip in 1712 for Sir Robert Atkyns' *Ancient and Present State of Gloucestershire* – a print of which has passed through the hands of successive owners of the house and hangs in the hall of the hotel today (see p. 142 and jacket).

The garden is very much in the formal manner of the time derived from French garden design and the smaller-scale gardens of the Netherlands. Elaborate detail, topiary, trees, ornamental shrubs (called 'greens') and water were all typical features of such schemes.

Lawrence's garden is not only a family memorial, it is designed symbolically. Such symbolism was also of the time but the Shurdington garden description gives the only known example where, as Lawrence wrote to Sir Thomas Lawrence (letter 51) 'the design appears not to the world unless I turn the key and discover the secret'. We are fortunate in having Lawrence's description to 'turn the key' for us too. The extraordinary attention to detail and the symbolism read strangely today but, conceived in the year of Anne's and Willy's deaths, indicate the intensity of his anguish and his need to 'eternise the memory of the dead and open to the next age my love and my grief'.

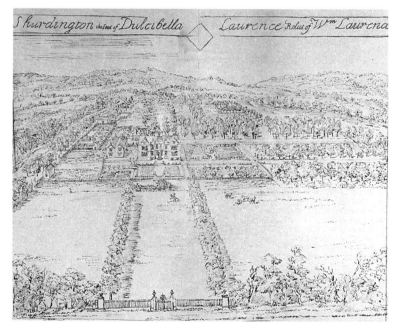

Probably the preparatory drawing by Johannes Kip for his print of
Shurdington in 1712

The Ancients erected to the honour of their deceased friends sometimes pillars and sometimes pyramids. I have unhappily lost many of my nearest relations, and especially two within the compass of two months, who were my two eyes, the brightest part of myself, a wife, and an only son. But that I may preserve as well in my eye as my heart the constant remembrance of their great merit, their untimely fate, and my own misfortune, I have raised these piers, which unite that double sort of monument, and equally participate of the pillar and the pyramid. The pillars are the bases upon which the pyramids rise gently from the bottom to the point, the middle part of them bearing the shape of urns, in which kind of repositories the ancient Romans laid up the bones and ashes of the dead.[1] In church monuments the body seems to lie in one grave and the tomb in another, for the tomb thus enclosed and covered with that sacred edifice lies like the body in a kind of obscurity, being seen by one parish only, and that but one day in seven. But by that which is done in this place and designed in another, not only the two great lights above shall daily see how my two below were basely extinguished; but all persons even to the extent of the horizon may, by observing and pitying their fall, prepare and expect their own. In the whole my fancy seems in very proper colours to have designed and drawn out the picture of human life.

The way to the three first of the smaller pair of pillars is narrow and without ornament, to show the immature, contracted, and barren condition of our infant years. Through this first gate you enter into the upper court before the house, which represents youth in a wider and more beautiful figure. And being past this second gate you enter into the garden, a large green plat, by which is signified our manly state, and the more large and florid enjoyments of life. Out of this and through the third gate you pass into the old orchard, and upon a long raised walk into the new: the former represents our declining age, and the latter our decrepit years, and therein the return of our childhood: for, very old men enter a second time into the cradle before they fall into the tomb; there being but little difference between infancy and decrepit old age, nisi quod haec rugosior et plures numerat natales [except that it is more wrinkled and counts more birthdays].*

In the midst of the garden stands the aged statue of Time, for he is called Κρόνος or Deus Temporis, he rests one hand upon a scythe, and with the other points to a row of cypress. At his foot on the one side is a wolf, representing Mars; for that beast was consecrated to that wild deity: on the other side is a snake or serpent, under which figure Æsculapius came to

*At the end of this long walk grows a yew tree, which seems to stop our futher progress and show the bounds of life.

1 These can be seen in the portrait of Anne on p. 80 and must either have been added to the portrait after her death – or the garden pyramids and urns were, perhaps, themselves derived from the portrait?

Rome, and was in that shape worshipped as a God.[2] On the right hand is a row of cypress, a tree always made use of in funeral pyres, and is therefore, by reason of its cold dark shade and bitter leaf, set here as an emblem of death. And below that is another garden, or plat of ground filled with dwarf trees of various fruits.

But to go on in the contemplative part. The many gates show the many obstacles we find in our pilgrimage, and how one misfortune is still succeeded by another. In like manner the coats of arms show the many bars and crosses we meet with before we come into the garden, that is, into our full age, and our best enjoyments of life. The gate which leads into this garden is answered by a third gate over against it of the same figure; and the crosses in it intimate, that our afflictions attend us to the very end of our race, and that our entrance into our manhood at one gate, and then by the side of a row of cypress even to our exit at the next, shows, that our whole passage through this mortal life is subject to so many accidents, that we totter at every step we make, and daily touch upon the cypress, the borders of death. As to the escutcheons in the two gates of the upper court they particularly point at those dear persons my wife and son: the red crosses as if dyed in the blood of our saviour, show their redemption; the white field their innocent lives; the black border, their lamented deaths; and the azure blue round the whole, their happy eternity. To which blessed place the pyramids lift up their points, and (quasi digito) as it were with a finger show us, that this dear couple possess what we should seek, and are already entered into that infinite circle of peace and glory.

The very prime and substantial part of life I represent (as I have said) by the garden plat, for just such is our state of manhood, it looks very smooth, fresh, gay and green, but like the grass that springs there, it soon begins to wither and decay. In the middle of this plat is erected the statue of Saturnus or Time, to show that it is time which gives measure and bounds to life and human felicity. His forelock shows the advice he gives; his scythe shows the slaughter he makes; he cuts down every individual of mankind, and must at last make an end of the whole species. He points to the cypress to show, that there lies the conclusive period as well to himself as the whole creation; when the world shall be reduced again into its original nothing. He, who was once edax rerum, [destructive of things][3] must then starve no more; death is his fate as well as ours; and if we and our heirs must be devoured by time, he and all his numerous issue of days, months, and years, must end in that which hath no end, and be at last swallowed up by eternity. The wolf and the serpent at the feet of Time are explained by this inscription upon the

2   There are several inaccuracies in the print from Kip's drawing – for instance, the statue of Time appears as a small tree. The Greeks identified Κρόνος (Cronos), the father of Zeus, with Χρόνος (Chronos), 'Time'.
3   Ovid, *Metamorphoses* 15, 234.

pedestal: multi Marte, plures Æsculapio, omnes Saturno; that is, many are mowed down by the war, more by the physician, all by time: the war kills, the physician murders, and time devours. And well might Æsculapius be worshipped under the shape of a snake or serpent, for, as I have tried to my double sorrow, many physicians are like that ungrateful snake in Æsop, which the unwary peasant took into his bosom, we warm them with our fees and they kill us with their physic. Nay, even Apollo the father of that faculty and first inventor of physic, had that name given him ἀπὸ τοῦ ἀπολλύειν A Destruendo [from the fact that he destroys]; for he first brought the plague into the world, and like our modern artists, killed much faster than he cured.

This green plat of manhood is bounded on the right hand with a row of cypress, that so if on the one side we think of our vigorous age and the pleasures of life, we may on the other side think of their period. Let us enjoy our years, but still remember our end, and how both we and they must have a sure and may have a sudden conclusion. Again, as the green plat represents the vigour of this life, so the garden below it, thronged with dwarf trees of various fruits, denotes the full and glorious enjoyments of the next.

The cypress trees, which run in a single line, and pass between them both, signify death, and show, that it is that little point alone which divides the present and the future life; it finisheth the temporal and begins our eternal being. Into which happy state God (at his pleasure) send me a quick and easy passage; for this mortal life is but a very bubble, and gives me no better wish than a cupio dissolvi [desire to perish]. It is supported awhile by our weak breath, as that thin bubble is by the included air, it swells and briskly swims about for a time, but the dart of Death easily pricks and breaks it. The bubbles dissolve,[4] those proud shells of air and water are lost and scattered in their first causes; they fall into the bosom of their primitive parents, and are no longer distinguished; only perhaps some new bubbles may start up in their places, but neither more solid nor more lasting. Just so 'tis with this bubble of life; we break away and without any future distinction dissolve into our first elements; we retire and are seen no more; only perhaps we leave behind us a new succession, another generation of bubbles, but these also inherit our frailty, and have neither a tougher skin nor a longer breath. They may move to and fro, and perhaps with pride enough, but must at last bow to the fate of their predecessors, and be not only lost but forgotten. Nay, these very monuments by which I endeavour to eternise the memory of the dead, and open to the next age my love and my grief, are but a more solid sort of bubbles, for a long race of years will consume 'um, and that which now riseth so high into the air, the corroding teeth of time will at last grind away and humble into dust. Data sunt ipsis quoque fata sepulcris [even tombs meet their ends].[5]

---

4   Bubbles were typically used by artists and poets of the time to symbolize transience.
5   Juvenal, *Satires* 10, 146.

My great-grandfather bought; my grandfather built; my uncle increased; I beautified; and my only son died without issue. These five descents are visible in the arms upon the five gates. The sixth gate, which leads out of the grove, and is in the rear of all the rest, hath only two round O's; to show, that the great pudder [pother] which we successively make to enlarge our possessions and perpetuate our families is but a vain attempt and comes at last to just nothing. God and the Law never favour perpetuities: He may often connive at the appetite of those who gather wealth for wealth's sake; but when they design to fasten it to their names and labour to make them both immortal, they by this excess of thought, invade the divine attribute, and then he breaks their measures, and without the methods of Law by some fatal stroke or other He destroys this chimera and cuts off this weak entail. For either the estate shall be wasted by a prodigal, or the name lost for want of males; or else by the distaff the former shall be transferred and the latter drowned in some other family: all which misfortunes have more than once been visible in the many descents of mine. Jugera quid faciant? quid prosit, Pontice, longo sanguine censeri? [What good are acres? What benefit, Ponticus, is being distinguished for a long ancestry?].[6]

The capital letters upon the several splints over the cornice of the pillars are particular remembrances and I preserve them for my own private contemplation.

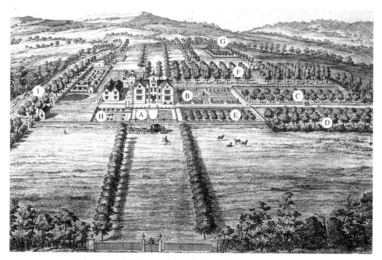

Johannes Kip's print of Shurdington in 1712.
A = upper court; B = plat; C = old orchard; D = new orchard; E = second plat of fruit trees; F = grove; G = fish pond; H = flower garden; I = the Greenway

6   An adaptation of Juvenal, *Satires* 8, 1–2.

In Continuation

The double gates of the first pair of piers bear the coats of my great-grandfather and grandfather; on the splint of the pillar dedicated to the former are these capital letters P.E. that is, Proavus Emit [my great-grandfather bought this]: he bought the Manor of Sherington in An: 3tio Eliz. [1516]. On the splint of the other pillar belonging to my grandfather are these. A.Æ that is, Avus Ædificat: he afterwards built the house. On the outside of the former splint is this remembrance. N. 15. O. 1518 and under it D. 10. N. 1582. On the outside of the other splint is this, N. 7. AV. 1565. and under it, D. 1638 showing the time of their birth and death. N. standing for Natus and D. for Denatus. On the east side of one pillar is a sundial with this motto ORIENTES. On the west side of the other pillar is another sundial with this motto OCCIDIMUS. which two joined together give us this memorandum Orientes Occidimus. for every east hath its west, every rise hath its set. While we are rocking in the cradle we are moving to the tomb and our first steps do but draw us nearer to our last. Every minute of life contracts it: we hasten to our end as soon as we begin: as soon as we begin to live we begin to die, nascentes morimur finisque ab origine pendet [being born we die and the end depends upon the beginning].

The second pair of piers are dedicated to my uncle, bearing his coat of arms in the middle of the folding gates. On the splint of one pillar are these letters P.A.E.A. that is, Patruus Auxit et Admisit: my uncle increased the estate and let me into the possession. On the splint of the other pillar are these, N. 20 May.1594. and under it D. 28 Aug: 1682. which show the time of his birth and death. Under the cornice of each pillar there is a sundial; over the one are these words ULTIMA. SEMPER. – over the other these, NEC. METUAS. NEC. OPTES. which in conjunction show, that we are always to expect our last day, but never to desire nor fear it.

The 3rd and 4th pair of piers in the upper court, as appears by their arms in the gates, are the particular monuments of my wife and son. Upon the splint of the first pillar dedicated to my wife are these capital letters, I.F.E.F.B.E.A.C. that is, Illa Fide, et Forma, Bonitate, et Acumine, Clara. [celebrated for her faith and beauty and goodness and wisdom]. On the second dedicated to my Son are these, D.E.I.C.I. that is, Dotibus eximiis Juvenum celeberrimus Ille [the most distinguished of young men for his outstanding gifts]. Under the cornice of the first pillar is a south dial with these words, LUX. ALMA. RECESSIT. that is, my fair light is departed. Under the cornice of the second pillar is the like dial with these words, ABSTULIT. ATRA. DIES. that is, black was that day which robbed me of my son. On the splint of the third pillar are these capital letters, C.C. that is, Carissimae Conjugi [to my dearest wife]. On the splint of the 4th are these, O.I. that is, Optimo Juveni [to an excellent young man]. On the inside of the former there is this remembrance, N. 24. AUG. 1650. and under it, D. 12 Jan.

1691[2]. On the inside of the latter is this, N. 19, JUN. 1668 and under it, D. 8 MAR. 1691. both inscriptions showing the time of their birth and death. The double gates of these piers bear on the inside my wife's coat, and my son's; but on the outside towards the garden they show my coat and my wife's: and so the outside of the 3rd pillar continues her monument, and the outside of the 4th stands for mine. On the splint of her pillar are these letters, T.Q.S.V.C. that is Tristeque sequar Vestigia, Conjux [and sadly shall I follow your footsteps, wife]. Death calls, and I shall quickly follow. Under the cornice is a south dial with this motto, LUMEN. ET. UMBRA. that is, Vita nihil nisi Lumen et Umbra [life is only light and shade]. Our lives are a composition of black and white; if in one hour they are bright and clear, in the next, they are dark and cloudy; and are indeed nothing but a mixed variety of light and shade. On the splint of the other pillar is this dedication, V.D. that is, Viro Dolorum; to the man of sorrows. Under the cornice is the like south dial, with this Motto, ANTE. OBITUM. NEMO. No man can be said to be happy till his latest minutes; 'til the sun be set, we can give no full account of the day: it is only the last hour that lets us see and judge of all the rest.

The 5th pair of piers are dedicated to the memory of my father and my brother; the double gates bear their arms and are distinguished by a crescent. On the splint of my father's pillar are these letters P.E.P. that is, Pio et Patienti. Piety and patience were his particular virtues. On the splint of my brother's pillar are these, V.V.G. that is, Viro veré Generoso: to the truly generous man. On the inside of the former splint is this remembrance, N. 18. SEP. 1606 and under it, D.6. DEC. 1678. on the inside of the latter is this,

$$\left.\begin{matrix} N \\ D \end{matrix}\right| \quad \text{FES. S.}^{TI}\text{ LAURENTII} \quad \left|\begin{matrix} 1638 \\ 1678 \end{matrix}\right.$$

[the feast of St Lawrence] pointing out the time of their birth and death.[7]

The first pair of piers which lead from the grove to the pond, have, on the top of the pillars and in lieu of the pyramids, only two large round O's. About the rim of one of them are these words, O. QUANTUM. EST. IN. REBUS. INANE. O how hollow and empty are all human enjoyments. About the rim of the other are these, OMNIA. VANITAS. All things are as vain and hollow as a cypher, which in itself is so insignificant that it makes neither price nor number. As all things began so all things must end; they all make but one round O, from nothing they came, and to nothing must return.

Upon the top of my house I designed a study for my son and finished it after his death.[8] Over it is a globe of flint glass of two foot diameter, with his red crest for a vane, (which is the body of the lucy or pike) and in it are cut

---

7 In the *Diary*, Lawrence gives Isaac's dates as 1639–79, which are confirmed by the letter to John Wright at the time of Isaac's death.

8 Again the print is inaccurate, showing the study as a square structure. It was, in fact, an octagonal cupula and can be seen in the drawing opposite. The 'globe of flint glass' Lawrence goes on to describe, no longer existed when the drawing was made *c.* 1910.

'Upon the top of my house I designed a study for my son . . .'

these letters, F.V.V.O. that is, Filio Unico Unigenito Optimo [to an excellent one and only son]. And (if it be not too fond a thought or too great a stretch of fancy) the sun glittering upon the glass seems to me to kindle a flame and burn incense to his memory. Two of the front windows as appears by the two crosses raguly, represent me and my son; the door between 'um, which is also a window of the same shape and opens into a balcony, represents my wife as appears by her coat which is argent, two bars gules: in all three the glass makes the field. This vane in the shape of a crest puts me in mind of the unsteady condition of families, how giddy they are, and how swiftly turned about by the many accidents of life, as this vane is by the change of wind. So that even in their highest elevation, they are subject to such trembling motions and shaking fits, that no rational thought can ever look upon them to be secure and fixed.

But that every place may present me with the objects of my loss, and perhaps to show that grief itself hath its vanity, I have made a flower garden. The walls of it within are of brick with pilasters of free-stone; the walls without are of free-stone with pilasters of brick. The piers have on the top a plain pyramid. On the one side of them is a jetting escutcheon of free-stone, with a cross raguly of brick for myself; on the other side is the like escutcheon bordered with black, and in it two bars of brick for my wife. So that the colours of both coats are natural white and red. On each side of these stands a laurel, not only by reason of its constant verdure, but because Laurentius a lauro dictus [Laurence derives from laurel]. The flower beds in this garden have a particular figure: the cross walks between them are in the shape of a cross raguly, and paved with brick. And in each quarter is an escutcheon with my wife's arms bordered with black; the field is of stone and the bars of brick. So that (as before) all the coats are represented in natural colours. Each of these four escutcheons is enclosed in a bordure of daisies; which being not only lasting flowers, and of a very pretty variety, but also very numerous and thick, I fancy to be but a crowd of eyes come to gaze upon her funeral.

But that the liquid element may also contribute to their memory, and that while I think of them on the land, I may not forget 'um on the water, the gate with the two round O's leads up to a square pond, about which is a double bordure of trees. In the middle of this pond is a square building with a balcony round it. On each side, and in the midst of the wreathed balusters is an escutcheon with two bars gules; the white wall behind it makes the field. The windows and doors on each side open with a cross raguly gules. On the top (and perhaps not improper for a fish-pond) stands erect, and as it were with the head plunged in the water, the crest of my family; which is the lucy or pike, with the head plunged in the helm. And that the remembrance of my losses may be visible as well within the water as above it, the water in a calm is so very smooth and clear, that it represents the building and with equal beauty. From this house as from a centre I am making four walks, whose trees on each side shall represent from the higher grounds a growing cross. A cross which if it can take good root and escape the axe, may outlive all the rest, and last many ages.

I had almost forgot that at the entrance into the narrow court, and in the wall of ashlar, there stands on each side an escutcheon of free-stone, like those on the garden wall. One of them hath in it two bars of brick: the other a cross raguly of brick. Their bordures of black show them to be the mourning monuments of my wife and son.

The next thing in design are six almshouses to be built on the rising of the hill, three on a side: between them will be an ascent of many steps to the top of a tump of about 30 foot square, whereon I intend to erect a chapel, which will stand in view of the whole vale and be seen from a distance of many miles. To this place I intend to remove the bodies, and in monumental figures give the finishing strokes of my love and fancy.

Lawrence did not live to complete the last part of his design. In his Will he had made provision for £1000 to be taken from the rents of the estate, at an annual rate of £100, to build the almshouses and chapel – but this was ignored. The avenue of trees in Kip's drawing leads only to the open space at the foot of the hill. Two yew trees still stand which were probably planted at the beginning of the avenue and at the edge of, what was then, the grove. The chapel apart, that Dulcibella should fail to build the almshouses does not tally with Lawrence's claim that she was 'obliging both to the rich and the poor'. It is possible that, with the number of calls on the estate, there was insufficient income to finance the scheme. Gloucestershire's prosperity, based on the wool and cloth trade, which had been at its height in the 16th century, was in decline and the new land and window taxes (to pay for the war) must have considerably reduced Dulcibella's income.

'generations pass while some tree stands and old families last not three oaks'
Sir Thomas Browne, *Urn Burial*
Some of the oaks planted by William Lawrence. The fishpond stood in
the midst of the trees, to the right, in the middle distance

The garden lay-out lasted no more than two generations. In the eighteenth century, following the landscape fashion in garden design, a ha-ha was built, curving through Lawrence's upper court and orchards. Today a few trees stand of his plan (of which, he had said, if they could 'take good root and escape the axe, may out-live all the rest, and last many ages'). The shape of the garden plat remains and a tangled piece of boggy ground where the fish pond once stood. The cupula, designed as a study for Willy, was taken down in recent years when it became unsafe and only the stump remains. Despite this, and later additions, the house is still very much as Lawrence knew it.

and paſſionate remembrance which you have of my deare Brother's untimely Fate; a loſs that ſtill ſhakes my very Being, and is enough to drive me into a contempt of all humane thinges. But that your remaining yeares may have a long extent and an eaſy period; and that we may live to ſee theſe riſing Stormes of ſtate gently expire and ſettle into a Calme, is (I am ſure) your Common prayer as well as mine, they dayly imploy, but can never tire the Devotion of

                                     Sr.   your affectionate Brother,

    1698   W. L.

                    For my Brother Iſaac Laurence at Argire.

Dear Brother,

Had I cloſely purſued the Reſpects due from Nature and Example I ſhould have return'd as many Letters as I have received, but the diſtance is ſo great, and the Conveyance ſo confuſ'd, that it is very hard to reach you. Argire hath been an old Enemy and almoſt alwayes in Armes againſt our Trade and our Religion; ſhe hath been guilty of a long pyracy, and her Shoares formerly polluted with the lamentable Shipwrack of the Spaniſh Navy; and to make the Scale more heavy I may throw in my owne wrongs; ſhe now robbs me of your Society, and ſteales away that Bleſſing to which I have a Natural as well as a Civil Right. By my laſt I ſent you the Newes then in being, and that you may ſee how a ſmall time may give birth to many great Revolutions, I give you a Satyrical Taſt of what hath happen'd ſince; and referre you to the print for a more ſolid Information.   The Army that military Hydra have made a dreadfull Change, and caſt the Affaires of the Nation into a new Mould; the Face of Government is ruin'd, the parliament diſſolv'd, and our new protector level'd again into his old private Fortune. They ſtand up for the good old Cauſe, as good indeed as old, for 'tis an Infant within Age, receiving its birth but in 41, when their Rage ran high, broke all the bonds of Law and Religion, and made Maieſty ſhamefully bleed and expire. This ſpurious Brat, this Sonne of Confuſion

The end of Letter 24 and the beginning of Letter 2 from William Lawrence's manuscript

Appendix B

The following is the complete text of the historical part of letter 2 which was abridged in Part I. The annotations already given are not repeated but, for interest, Lawrence's own spelling has been retained.

LETTER 2

May 30th 1659

. . . By my last I sent you the Newes then in being, and that you may see how a small time may give birth to many great Revolutions, I give you a Satyrical Tast of what hath happen'd since, and referre you to the Print for a more solid Information.[1]

The Army that military Hydra hath made a dreadfull Change, and cast the Affaires of the Nation into a new Mould; the Face of Goverment is ruin'd, the Parliament dissolv'd, and our new Protector level'd again into his old Private Fortune. They stand up for the good Old Cause, as good indeed as old, for 'tis an infant within Age, receiving its birth but in 48, when their Rage ran high, broke all the bonds of Law and Religion, and made Majesty shamefully bleed and expire. This spurious Brat, this Sonne of Confusion, was nurs't up for foure yeares, and then turn'd out for an impertinent useless thing: after this it wandred about the Nation like a Vagabond meeting neither with Pitty nor Relief; at last the poore Foole being almost starv'd and under the lash of a severe Goverment, fled to the Army for Protection; whose Officers full of Guilt and Feares, receive this sorry Brat this Good Old Cause, fed and cloath'd him in many gay Colours, gave him a House to live in and some carefull Tutours, whom they call by the name of the Long Parliament. They would perswade the world that he is very gentle and innocent, but to me he lookes as fierce as a Cannibal; for thinges seeme to be in a very tragick condition, tending to Blowes and Blood, and hastily running into their first Confusion.

The Nation is so trampled upon by Troopers, and so submissive to the force of Powder, that every single Nine-penny Redcoate thinkes he can discharge a Parliament with as much ease as his Musquet. Faux's Treason seems to be now reviv'd; what he design'd, these execute; he prepar'd a Blow, but these give it. In this they agree, they both put their Powder in Barrels; but then in this they differ, the army acts with a much greater

---

1   Probably from the licensed 'Weekly Intelligencer'.

impudence; for he work't in the darke, but these at noone-day; he modestly hid his Powder, but these shake their barrels and openly show it. 'Tis well they are shut up in a Island for else they would shake the whole body of Nature, and put the Universal Frame into Disorder and Confusion. The Praetorian Bandes, the Mamalukes, the Janissaries were like to those Souldieres in all thinges but their Pride and Insolence, in which they are not to be equall'd unless by their more natural Protector the Governor of Hell, that strong Garrison of Redcoates. There is nothing like a blush in the whole Army but their Coates, I beleeve they are out of God's Protection, and that when he lookes upon the Nation he holds his hand between his Eye and the Army, else such successive Sinnes could not lye so long unreveng'd.

But under the shelter of this lewd Army, this Rump of a Parliament are got into their former Seates: if God shall be with them, it is for no other reason but because there are two or three met together; fifteen Votes pass't the first day: I beleeve that in a fortnight we may have Ordinances enough to furnish a Navy.[2] They have voted down Authority in a single Person; best of all, for now they may fall to their old Practice of Piety, and grease and gratify one another; vote an Estate to me to-day, and I'le doe as much for you to morrow. They have scatter'd the Church and Crowne Revenues, have ruin'd many Families to raise their owne, and yet will vote on still, and never put an end to their Avarice and Ambition.[3] Under the pretence of abolishing the very Markes and Remembrance of Royalty, they have voted the sale of Whitehall,[4] but the intent is that it may be divided and sold to one another at easy rates, and they have already given the Palace of St James's to Fleetwood for his Arreares,[5] and will doe the like to others that they may the better fasten and secure their Usurpation. The British Oake being hew'd down, they make hast to dispose of all his Branches; and if their Hearts were but as open as their Violence, we should easily see that this sort of Rapine is that Good Old Cause which they so dote upon and make their Idol.

There have been of late yeares so many Changes and such Antipodes in Goverment, that I think no Age or Nation hath been so eminently wicked as to be able to produce a Parralel; and yet there are still such abundance of ill-

---

2 A pun on Parliamentary decrees and armaments.

3 Bishops, Dean and Chapters had been abolished and their incomes, intended for the clergy, went to pay government creditors. The property of Roman Catholic and Cavalier landlords was also sequestered.

4 On 16th May, it had been resolved to bring a Bill before the House for the sale of Whitehall (and Somerset House) 'for and towards the satisfaction of the great Arreares and Pay due unto the Army'. (*House of Commons Journal*, Vol. VII, pp. 655–6.)

5 The coffeehouse gossips had exaggerated here. On the 13th May, the command and custody of 'St James Park by Whitehall' (not the Palace) had been committed to General Fleetwood. (*House of Commons Journal*, Vol. VII, p. 650.) It was not such an improbable idea – General Lambert had previously been given Queen Henrietta Maria's palace at Wimbledon.

William Prynne

humours in the Fanatick heads of our new Masters, and the Disease so very averse to a solid cure, that I feare a Veine must be once more open'd, and we must at last bleed into a better temper.

This Junto [Council] at Westminster seemes to be an Assembly of Dippers,[6] a fine precise Congregation: they set up for Perfection, will admit of no open Sinners, and hate all visible Pollution. They have turn'd out Harry Martin for a Whoremaster,[7] and refused Pryn, either because his Head was circumcis'd or because he smelt of the older and better Cause.[8] He reassumes his first Presbyterian fury and raves like a Madman: he tires the press with his Pamphlets, whets his teeth against the Good Old Cause, and bites as close as a Badger, but all this and more he may doe securely, for he knowes how to put a cheate upon the Pillory. To admonish him by an Aurem Vallere [tweaking of the ears][9] is of no use, his Eares are gone and he will heare of no accomodation. He lookes upward as smooth as a Bowle, and that bitter Party never had a Rounder Head.

But yet I wonder why Martin should be expell'd for being carnally inclined, and Atkins[10] that Babel of Flesh be receiv'd, who is generally

6 A name given to Baptists and Anabaptists. (*OED*)

7 When Cromwell dissolved the Rump Parliament in 1653, he accused several members of being 'whoremasters'. Henry Marten, an ardent Republican, was the particular object of this accusation.

8 i.e. those who sought to curb the powers of the Crown but not to destroy it. William Prynne, as a Presbyterian, was one of those refused admittance to the re-formed Rump Parliament on 8th May. As a tireless pamphleteer, he was first in trouble for criticizing Charles I's Queen, Henrietta Maria, for appearing in Court masques and, by order of the Star Chamber, was fined, pilloried and had his ears cut off. One of his publications criticized men for wearing long hair, (his own hair was short – the origin of the term 'roundhead' – but just covered his missing ears).

9 cf. Vergil, *Eclogues* 6, 3–4.

10 Probably Thomas Atkyns, typically the object of such comment, M.P. for Norwich 1645–60, and Lord Mayor of London 1644–5.

knowne to be the looser liver. . . . — [Un-named] had not a wider Paunch, his set of Fingers look like so many Christmas Candles, and are so swell'd with Fat, that it is no wonder how Gold comes to be so scarce, every Ring he weares being two sizes bigger then a Horse-Collar. Sure our wary Senate consider'd their small number and took in his spreading Carcase only to fill their empty House, and yet . . . to place him in the route of an Army or near the great Guns at a Muster is by his owne experience found to be a sure way to melt his grease:[11] A Stink is the Anagram of his name, thus he hath lived and thus he must dye. But to conclude this subject; this mock Parliament consists altogether of Members; from whence it be easily inferr'd, where all are Members there is no Head; where there is no Head there are no Braines; and where there are no Braines judg you if we are not like to have a wise Goverment.

They have made the Protector less then a Roy d'Yvedot, and strip't him of all his Honours; his Fortune halts as well as he. Usurped Dominions must be kept by the same means they were acquir'd; his Father left him his Throne but not his Courage; he was loss't for want of Resolution, and his loss is therefore the greater, because 'tis thought that upon consideration of a legal Right in a restless Party and that no violent thinges are perpetual, he was inclin'd to satisfy the hopes of many by a faire Resignation. Weeping Fleetwood was perswaded to head the Revolution, he hath the greater Power but Lambert the greater Craft, who 'tis said, endeavors to possess all, by the more secret arts of Divide and Raigne: which is a principle which may perhaps serve a present turne, but must at last undoe the whole Party.

If you ask me what are become of our Lords and Merchants of the Upper House, I'le tell you, that Trading was growne extreamly dead there, they had nothing to doe, and did Nothing, and so broke and had their Shop shut up.[12] The Souldieres indeed for want of pay were so contracted with hunger, that one might have drawne half the Army through one of Atkins Rings; and therefore it was no wonder to see them turne out those new Lords, when their minds ran so extreamly after Commons.[13] Whaley, Goff, and Ingolsby, have loss't both their Honours and Authority, they made some small showes of Repentance, and therefore were discarded by the Army-Gamesters, who have shuffled, cut, and dealt the cards so well, that they have now got the whole Game into their owne handes.[14]

11 This reference is obscure, but the implication – that Atkyn's courage was as small as his person was large – is clear enough.
12 The House of Lords had been abolished by the Rump Parliament of 1648 but re-formed, as a nominated 'Upper House' (so called because most of its members were not Peers), in 1658.
13 A pun on the House and army rations (as in to be 'on short commons').
14 Major-General Edward Whalley (Cromwell's cousin), Major-General William Goffe and Colonel Richard Ingolsby, who were not thought to be sufficiently zealous for the 'Good Old Cause'. All were signatories of Charles I's death warrant.

Alderman Titchburne another of our homespun Lords,[15] saw which way the wind blew; he quickly closeth with the Army and promiseth to stand by them in whatsoever they should undertake; you may measure his Conscience by the extent of his Promise: he can serve the Times so well, and turne with such abundance of dexterity, that I am of opinion that his Soule is nothing but a Chamelion rarify'd, or that he is of the race of the Spanish Gennets and was got by a Wind.[16] His Gold Chaine which he thinkes an Ornament may prove a Presage; he was one of those who committed that barbarous murder in 48 [of Charles I] and the sentence which the Law pronounces even in common Murders is to be hang'd in Chaines; and I hope it will be his Fate to dye in his owne. He is a pretty timber'd Lad and without question would swing neatly: the man hath deserv'd well, is ready at every turne, and therefore 'tis pitty but his Turne should be serv'd first.

The Merchants break apace. Estates at Sea must needes receive much dammage when there are so many Stormes at Land. Excise and Customes eate up the gaines both of Land and Sea, Taxes swallow up the Gentry and the Souldieres all. Religion is nothing but a Pretence, and he that can be the best Hypocrite shall be the greatest man. Lawyers and Divines are under a cloud, being thought to have reach't at a King and Bisshops: perhaps the Army will now cancel both Law and Gospel, for that is the nearest way to Liberty of Conscience. Our Courts of Judicature must be new modell'd and while the Army rules the new Judges must be fitted to the Cause,[17] and must rather use the Sword then the Scales of Justice.[18]

It will be three yeares before I can reach the Barre, and therefore I don't much care though the Pockets of the Subject be poore and their Tongues at Peace: but when that time is expir'd, I shall begin to pray that God would send much mony and many Quarrels. . . .

15 Alderman Sir Robert Titchborne was a member of the nominated Upper House and a signatory of Charles I's death warrant. He was knighted by Cromwell in 1656 and made Lord Mayor of London the same year.
16 The reference to Spanish Gennets (a small mediterranean mammal) is unclear. 'Begot by a wind' is a mythological reference – perhaps, in this case, unkindly suggesting that Alderman Titchborne's parentage was less than orthodox.
17 On the 9th May, a Bill 'concerning Proceedings in Courts of Law and Equity' was given its first reading but a vote the following day rejected a second reading. (*House of Commons Journal*, Vol. VII, p. 647.)
18 Apparently a reference to a committee of 25, 11 of whom were army officers, who were appointed to bring in an Act of Indemnity and Pardon 'for what hath been acted or done, during these late Times'. (*House of Commons Journal*, Vol. VII, pp. 654–5.)
  Both in this, and in the 'new modelling' of the Courts, the information seems to be based on a garbled account of the Commons proceedings. Immediately prior to the setting up of the committee, four new Judges had been appointed, but none were military men.

Charles I's death warrant

FINAL POST-SCRIPT

For the reader interested in the fate of the chameleon-like **Alderman Robert Titchborne**: at the trial of the 29 Regicides remaining in 1660 (some, like Cromwell, had died; some had fled abroad) he claimed it was his 'unhappiness to be called to so sad a work when I had so few years over my head . . . '. 'I would have chosen a Red-hot oven to gone into as soon as that Meeting' (when the King's death warrant was signed). He was found guilty but with a recommendation for mercy and was one of those whose life was spared under the Act of Indemnity in 1660. He was imprisoned for life and died in the Tower of London in 1682. (*State Trials and 12 Charles II, cap II, clause XXXV*).

William Prynne continued to write pamphlets in the Presbyterian cause for which, in 1661, he was again denounced as a 'seditious rebel'. He became Keeper of Public Records in the Tower of London and died in 1669.

If William Prynne had lived to be involved in the Popish Plot years, he would have been in his element: he thought Quakers, and even Oliver Cromwell, were Jesuit agents in disguise.

Richard Cromwell, who had fled abroad in 1659, was allowed to return *c.* 1680 and lived in retirement until his death in 1712.

General Monk was created Duke of Albemarle, Master of the Horse, and continued to command the Army until his death in 1670.

General Fleetwood was first condemned and then reprieved; outlived his wife, Bridget (Cromwell's daughter); remarried – but was never again allowed to hold public office. He died in 1692.

General Lambert had his death sentence commuted by the King; spent 20 years in prison (pursuing his hobby of gardening) and died, senile, in 1684.

King Charles II had said to his First Minister, the Earl of Clarendon: 'I must confess I am weary of hanging except on new offences. Let it sleep. You know that I cannot forgive them.'

Index